T0354387

ENCYCLOPEDIA
CORRUPTION
IN THE WORLD

Book 5: Tools to Fight Corruption in
Mercosur and in the World

JUDIVAN J. VIEIRA

authorHOUSE®

AuthorHouse™
1663 Liberty Drive
Bloomington, IN 47403
www.authorhouse.com
Phone: 1 (800) 839-8640

Published by AuthorHouse 11/15/2018

ISBN: 978-1-5462-5528-4 (sc)
ISBN: 978-1-5462-5526-0 (hc)
ISBN: 978-1-5462-5527-7 (e)

Library of Congress Control Number: 2018909735

Print information available on the last page.

Thanks to:

My mother (in memoriam), who told me when I was still the assistant of a bricklayer that studying would make a difference in my life.

Eliane Caetano, an advisor and head of my personal office for efficiency and help in the research phase and bibliographic organization, during the five years that made this work a scientific reality and an innovative proposal.

Neither the corrupt nor the virtuous has power over their moral behavior, but they had, rather, power to become one thing or another; so also someone who throws a stone has power over it before hurling it, but does not have it after having thrown it.

Aristotle

CONTENTS

Introduction..xi

Chapter 1   Constitutional Symmetries in Mercosur.........................1

    1.1 - Political-legal symmetries in Mercosur............................8

    1.1.1 - Table 1 – The Republican form.....................................8

    1.1.2 - Table 2 - The representative system and the
        democratic regime of government.................................9

    1.1.3 - Table 3 - All are State of rule in Mercosur...................10

Chapter 2   Hierarchy of International Treaties in The
        Constitutions of Mercosur...15

    2.1 Table: The hierarchy of the treaties in Constitutions
        of Mercosur...20

Chapter 3   Constitutional References on Corruption in Mercosur......47

    3.1 - Table with constitutional references on corruption
        in Mercosur...49

Chapter 4   Constitutional References on Creation of a
        Supranational Criminal Court in the Mercosur.............50

    4.1 - Table 1 – Existing Constitutional references on the
        creation of a supranational court in Mercosur..............59

    4.2 - Table 2 – Existing Constitutional references on the
        acceptance of a supranational legal order in Mercosur....60

    4.3 – Norms that have immediate and obligatory
        application in the scope of Mercosur.............................71

Chapter 5   Some Brazilian Penal and Administrative Paradigms 92

    5.1 Specific law on the act of improbity in Mercosur 92

    5.2 Financial Action Task Force against of Money
        Laundry (FATF) 100

Chapter 6   Proposal of the Unification of the Legislation to
        Combat Corruption 104

    6.1 - Crimes whose effects go beyond borders of each
        country member of Mercosur 106

Chapter 7   Concept of Public Official in the Scope of Mercosur 109

    7.1 - According to Inter-American Convention against
        Corruption (IACAC): 109

    7.2 - According to United Nations Convention against
        Corruption (UNCAC): 110

    7.3 - According to the International Legal Doctrine 111

    7.4 - In Criminal Code of Argentina 112

    7.5 - In Criminal Code of Brazil 113

    7.6 - In Public Service Law of Paraguay 114

    7.7 - In Constitution and Penal Code of Uruguay 114

    7.8 - In Criminal Code of Venezuela 115

Chapter   Unification or Integration in Mercosur:
        What is it about? 116

Final Considerations 127

Bibliography 131

INTRODUCTION

Coming to the end does not always mean exhausting the content of a given object. We come to the last of the five books convinced that Franz Kafka (2000: 32) is right when he says:

> "No story can be truly completed just as the truth of every thing, however persecuted by science in this evolving universe can be finally exhausted. There will always be a trail to go, which will lead to thousands of new considerations."

It is our wish that the academic community, politicians, legal practitioners and public managers read this work and receive it as a contribution made in the strict public interest and in the appreciation we give to substantial democracy.

Our dream is still to see a Republic where love for people is the engine of development.

On the long road to knowledge there are countless signs and warnings along the way. Life is alive. She communicates. Can you see and understand the signs?

Those who find time to interpret the signs and warnings tend to better understand the why, even though our senses are limited, our reason is weak, and our biological life brief, as Cicero has stated, with mastery in his book "The Offices" (p. 16-17).

The old orator came to the end of life more reflective than ever. He recalled the work of students in the Socratic, Platonic, and Aristotelian schools and stressed the importance of those who understood that reflecting on everything and everybody, may be the safest route to knowledge.

Cicero recalled how vague the attitude of those who passively accepted the prevailing views and, he added (Cicerón, Los Oficios: 15):

"That nothing should be dogmatically affirmed, but in every case to suspend our judgment; and instead of affecting certainty, we should be still with opinion based on verisimilitude, which is all that a rational understanding can assent to."

All living animals received instincts, but man was favored with reason. That is why must always investigate and with, as much depth as possible, the causes and consequences of conduct.

To live in society presupposes the exercise of reason, since it leads to self-knowledge.

What we were, we are, and the person we can become as human being, is a written formula in the cannones of History. Usually this knowledge is available in the books and in the councils that surround us. Do you read? Do you use to listen to the voice of the good advices?

Ethics and morality are not fads that from time to time deserves our attention. The survival of man on earth and elsewhere in the universe requires that living in society be permeated by those values.

If we exchange what is just for what is useful, and make it conscious and in free will, we must do so without forgetting that the Just is more dign and, no matter what we do, if we are conscious and free, we are responsible for the consequences of our act of commission or omission which we direct to specifi end.

Of curse, the corrupt prefers the useful because his inner being wants the immdiate rewards of life, regardless of the social inequality it can create. was with great ethical sense that Aristotle said "Neither the corrupt or the virtuous has power over their moral behavior, but they had, ratr, power to become one thing or another; so also someone who throws tone has power over it before hurling it, but does not have it after having rown it".

The corrupt purposely ignores that the peaceful coexistence of the groups which we exist, depends on respect for the limits established by ethics, orality and law.

I e that in this last volume we keep going on our journey of knedge, with the open mind and with the joy that the multiple world-views give us. Have you learned to respect the pluralism of life and knowledge? Knowledge can save us. It is exactly the opposite of the ignorance. That's why in the way of science and prosperity, ignorancre is not a blessing. Ignorance is a plague!

We cite historical, philosophical, and political-juridical truths in English, Spanish, and Italian, because I know that you came to this reading environment knowing, as Aristotle said, that "Being says itself in many ways" (The thinkwea, volumwe I, page. 24).

I add that, with some citations in the original language, I just wish you do not miss the essence of what was said, as sometimes occurs with the translation.

In this last book of this Encyclopedia, we ratify our call for the existence of sufficient symmetry for the unification of criminal, procedural penal and administrative-disciplinary legislation in Mercosur's legal systems, to combating corruption that materializes itself in crimes and acts of improbity that goes beyond borders of each country member of Mercosur.

I believe we could do the same, in certain measure, in other economics blocks such as BRICS and NAFTA. We still have European Union as a paradigm. If we don't want to do it to avvoid or justify our nationalism, so, at least, we should unify the criminal, procedural penal, and administrative-disciplinary legislation, even to avvoid the long waiting period in extraditions, due to the differences in our multiple criminal procedural systems.

I have full conviction that the guiding political-juridical principles of this research are universal. That is the reason why, what is said here applies to any country in the world, for we are not only based upon law, but Ethics and Morality, which are higher values.

We dare, with three proposals that we present in this Encyclopedia, namely:

1– We propose the unification of criminal, procedural penal and administrative-disciplinary legislation within the scope of Mercosul, together with the creation of a court with jurisdiction to prosecute crimes and acts of improbity against Mercosur Public Administrations;

2– We propose the creation of the Special Administrative Court with jurisdiction in Brazil, similar to what exists in Italy; and

3– We propose that crimes and acts of improbity, that is, that corruption with public income and public goods in general, be elevated to the category of crime against humanity, since such conduct kills more than wars, guerrillas and acts of terrorism around the world.

In the end, we have no doubt that the determinant of the changes that produce development leaps for a people is the political-legal will to produce substantial democracies. If there is no such will, it is left to the people to exercise their legitimate right of resistance against acts of corruption and corrupt systems of government.

Good reflection.

CHAPTER 1

Constitutional Symmetries in Mercosur

Before starting this chapter, we think it important to remember that the Mercosur region, in terms of democracy and exception regimes, has been like the pendulum of a driven clock by the following ideology: power conquered by force is only maintained by force and only comes out by force. (*in* The Essence of Power, 2001).

Norman Angell (2002: 190-191) records that a few years ago an Italian lawyer named Tomasso Caivano wrote a letter with memories and impressions of twenty years in Venezuela and the contiguous republics, and that his conclusions are worth mentioning, because they keep truths about almost every country in the region.

Tomasso Caivano, on bidding farewell to the Venezuelans, exhorted them by saying:

> "The curse that weighs upon you is the soldier and the character of the soldier. It is impossible, for two of you in particular, and even more so for two of your parties to hold a debate without wanting to fight for the cause in dispute, Venezuelans consider it an abdication of their dignity whatever it means to take into account the point of the other party to try to adjust to it, as long as it is possible to fight it using force. Personal courage seems to compensate for all defects. The military in bad faith is more considered in your society than the civilian of good qualities; military prowess and adventures are considered more honorable than honest work. The worst corruption is forgiven, as well

1

as the most grievous, as long as your leaders know how to clothe them with the tinsel of bluster and declamations about bravery, fate, and patriotism. Until there is a radical change in your spirit, you will continue to be victims of oppression. As long as the mass of your people-peasants and workers-do not refuse to allow yourself to be dragged into slaughter in quarrels that do not interest you, and which you only let yourself go because you prefer war to work, your beautiful territory, more fruitful than God has given to men, will not have a prosperous and happy people, enjoying the fruits of their labor in peace and joy."

Despite the adoration of some Latin American peoples for guns and dictatorships, the best way to resolve conflicts is still through debate, and the debate is field of democracy.

Fortunately, new winds of democracy have blown on Latin America, despite the tsunami of corruption that civilian governments have been imposing on region's people.

It is a moment of reflection on past mistakes, so that the Brazilian and Latin American people can evolve from the formal democracies in which we live, to substantial democracies in which human dignity is a reality and not a heap of crystallized promises in Constitutions of merely programmtic rules, such as we have in our present states of rule.

The globalization of information, the increase in life expectancy, and the slow gradual growth of the economy have fueled the awareness and growth the self-esteem of the peoples of this region so rich in natural and human resources.

However, the educational process of our peoples, which has been purposely tampered by utilitarian governments of the left and the right who blame each other to justify their disastrous passage through power, has been obstacle to the construction of the social dignity that we aim.

In Brazil, at the end of the 1980s we began to harvest the fruits of democracy dreamed of in, after so many exceptional dictator regimes. Unhappily the corruption on civil governments is a menace to de continuity of the democracy of the region.

One of the political-juridical dialogues proposed and initiated in this new was the regionalization of the economy and law, as tools for the construction of the social welfare of our peoples.

The idea of a Southern Common Market arises, following the example of the- European Union (EU) and NAFTA - North American Free Trade Agreement.

David Baigun and Nicolás Garcia Rivas made the following synthesis on the subject:

"In the words of the Brazilian constitutionalist Paulo Napoleão Nogueira da Silva, MERCOSUR is a reality that proposes to be much more than a simple free trade area, it is proposed to be a customs union, a true economic confederation that includes the possibility of adopting a single currency. In a critical perspective, Gabriela Wurcel indicates that, beyond the official name (Common Market of the South), it is far from being a true common market or a perfect customs union.

As Oscar Hermida Uriarte recalls, MERCOSUR has its origin in the Treaty of Asunción, celebrated on March 26, 1991 between Argentina, Brazil, Paraguay and Uruguay, regulating a period of transition or construction of a free trade zone between the four countries and a common external tariff in the bloc's relations with the rest of the world. By the Protocol of Ouro Preto of December 17, 1994, its definitive institutional structure was established, MERCOSUR being constituted in a "free trade zone" within it with an interregional tariff of 0%, with exceptions, and a "customs union" "Towards third countries with a differential common external tariff that ranges from 0 to 20%, with exceptions. According to the aforementioned Wurcel, the crisis that crossed the regional bloc at the end of the last millennium, even led to talk about the desirability of putting all the effort into consolidating, at least, the free trade zone, leaving aside the improvement of the customs union.

Adriana Dreyzin de Klor points out that by opting the bloc's rulers for a common market, the intergovernmental structure on which it is built has operational repercussions in all fields, not only the legal-structural one, the most critical being the lack of legislative bodies with competence legitimate to elaborate the right that governs its destiny, together with the lack of a Permanent Court of Justice. The verification of numerous disagreements among the members has been installed as an idea with consensus to make an institutional turnaround that gives the scheme a democratic legitimacy that it lacks. The current conflict between Argentina and Uruguay over the issue of paper mills in front of the province of Entre Ríos, is a clear example of the problems mentioned.

Since 1992, with an initial plan of four meetings, which began when the 1st International Seminar on "Regionalization of Criminal Law in MERCOSUR" was held in Asunción, Paraguay, between July 1 and 4, with the Participation of delegations from the four signatory countries, made up of recognized teachers of the subject, has been carried out different activities on the point. In that meeting, the topics addressed were: 1) judicial organization; 2) the movements of penal procedural reform and the protection of human rights; 3) cooperation procedures in criminal matters. The 2nd Seminar was held in Maldonado, Uruguay, from November 10 to 13, 1993, while the 3rd was held in Porto Alegre, Brazil, from October 27 to 29, 1994, and issues related to the international cooperation and issues related to economic criminal law. The 4th Seminar was held in Santa Fe, Argentina, from June 26 to 29, 1996, where topics related to economic crime were deepened, such as the criminal protection of competition, the penal regime of trademarks, patents and industrial designs and the comparative analysis of judicial systems and procedural guarantees in the area.

In August 2004, the Permanent Court of MERCOSUR was inaugurated in Asunción, the body in charge of resolving disputes concerning commercial disputes between the member countries, composed of five jurists;

4

it is a permanent arbitration body born at the proposal of Argentina (February 2002) that will be reflected in the Protocol of Olivos. It can act as a court of single instance between the States parties or in two instances (one "ad-hoc" and another as a Permanent Court of Review, in cases referring to problems of a commercial nature).

As for the structure of MERCOSUR, it is as follows:

1. Decision-making bodies:

a) Common Market Council: supreme body, has the political leadership and decision making. It is made up of the four presidents of the member countries, plus the four foreign ministers, the four finance ministers and the four presidents of the central banks.

b. Common Market Group: executive body. It is composed of four regular members and four alternate members for each country.

c. MERCOSUR Trade Commission: ensures the application of trade policy instruments. It is composed of four members and four alternate members for each country.

2 Parliamentary representation bodies:

* Joint Parliamentary Commission: represents the Parliaments of the States-party in MERCOSUR, seeks the harmonization of legislations as required by the integration process.

3. Advisory bodies:

Economic-Social Consultative Forum: makes recommendations to the Common Market Group

4. Support bodies:

* MERCOSUR Secretariat (permanent headquarters in Montevideo): operational support body, which deals with the provision of services to the other MERCOSUR bodies.

In order to close this synthetic news, it must be borne in mind that there is a democratic commitment between MERCOSUR and the Republics of Bolivia and Chile, embodied in the Ushuaia Protocol of 24/7/98, which had as its direct antecedent the "Presidential Declaration" and the adhesion protocol "signed in San Luis, on 6/25/96. There is also an "Agreement on extradition between the States Parties of MERCOSUR and the Republic of Bolivia and the Republic of Chile." Venezuela has recently announced its vocation to be the fifth full member, initiating the formalities (which concluded, closed this work, by the Protocol of accession of Caracas, signed on 4/7/06). There is also a "Protocol of mutual legal assistance in criminal matters of MERCOSUR", an "Agreement on extradition between the States parties of MERCOSUR" and progress has been made in the establishment of a unified retirement regime. (BAIGUN, David, RIVAS, Nicolás García (ed.), Economic Crime and Corruption, 1. ed. Buenos Aires: Hiar, 2006. pp. 280-284)."

We all point out from the collated synthesis the follow proposals for Mercosu

- be a free trade zone between the four countries, a common market;
- a "customs union";
- be, as a common market, the intergovernmental legal-structural structure;
- be an institutional turnaround that gives the scheme a democratic legitimacy to solve the conflicts of the region (e.g., what happened between Argentina and Uruguay because of the issue of paper mills in the province of Entre Ríos);

The implementation of this devir would pass through the regionalization of Criminal Law in MERCOSUR, following the following measures:

1) Judicial organization;
2) The movements of criminal procedure reform and the protection of human rights;
3) Cooperation procedures in criminal matters.

From the synthesis on the creation of the economic bloc, the authors highlight the following proposals for Mercosur to be a practical reality:

1– That a free trade zone be established among the member countries;
2– That it be a customs union;
3– That the intergovernmental legal and structural structure be the common market; and
4– That it be an institutional change that promotes democratic legitimacy for the solution of the region's conflicts, such as that between Argentina and Uruguay, due to the factory in the province of Entre Ríos.

In the end, David Baigun and Nicolás Garcia Rivas conclude that the implementation of this development goes through the regionalization of criminal law in Mercosur, with the parallel adoption of the following measures:

1) Judicial organization;
2) Criminal procedural reforms and protection of human rights;
3) Adoption of cooperation procedures in criminal matters

After conducting a comparative study of the Law of Mercosur member countries, we remain convinced of the possibility not only of integration in specific areas such as the EU and NAFTA do, as the possibility of taking a step forward through the unification of criminal, procedural penal and administrative–disciplinary rules that deal with crimes and acts of improbity against the Mercosur Public Administrations.

More of that, we propose a criation of a permanent Court of Justice with jurisdiction for the prosecution and judgment of the respective infractions that goes beyond borders of each member countries.

1.1 - Political-legal symmetries in Mercosur

We have already pointed out that symmetry is the relation of size or disposition that the things or parts must have with the whole. Political-legal symmetry was the focus of many debates among members of the Supreme Courts of Mercosur.

In some cases, their existence in other do not. That is why we set out to carry out a comparative study in the legislation of Mercosur member countries, with the aim of identifying the points of symmetrical convergence of our republican form, the representative system and the democratic regime of government, according to the Mercosur constitution.

The conclusions that we present do not leave doubt of the existence of political-legal symmetry. Here they are:

1.1.1 - Table 1 — The Republican form

ARGENTINA	Article 1º - The Argentine Nation adopts for its government the federal republican representative form, according to the present Constitution.
BRASIL	Art.	The Federative Republic of Brazil, formed by the interdependent union of the States and Municipalities and the Federal District, is constituted as a Democratic State of Law and has as its foundation:
PARAGUAI	Article 1 - IN THE FORM OF STATE AND GOVERNMENT: The Republic of Paraguay is forever free and independent. It is constituted as a Social State of law, unitary, indivisible, and decentralized in the manner established by this Constitution and the laws. The Republic of Paraguay adopts representative, participatory and pluralist democracy for its government, founded on the recognition of human dignity.
URUGUAI	Article 1. - The Oriental Republic of Uruguay is the political association of all the inhabitants included within its territory.

VENEZUELA	*Article 1. Venezuela declares itself Bolivarian Republic, irrevocably free and independent and bases its moral patrimony and its values of liberty, equality, justice and international peace, in the doctrine of Simon Bolivar, the Liberator.*

1.1.2 - Table 2 - The representative system and the democratic regime of government

ARGENTINA	The system of government in Argentina adopts the representative, republican and federal form (National Constitution, Art. 1). The people directly elect their representatives
BRASIL	Art. 1 The Federative Republic of Brazil, formed by the inseparable union of the States and Municipalities and the Federal District, is a Democratic State of Law (...) Art. 14. Popular sovereignty shall be exercised by universal suffrage and by direct and secret voting, with equal value for all, and, according to the law
PARAGUAI	Article 1 - IN THE FORM OF STATE AND GOVERNMENT: The Republic of Paraguay adopts representative, participatory and pluralist democracy for its government, founded on the recognition of human dignity.
URUGUAI	Article 77. - Every citizen is a member of the sovereignty of the Nation; as such, he is elector and eligible in the cases and forms that will be designated. The suffrage will be exercised in the manner determined by the Law, but on the following bases:
VENEZUELA	Article 6. The government of the Bolivarian Republic of Venezuela and the political entities that make up is and will always be democratic, participatory, elective, decentralized, alternative, responsible, pluralist and revocable mandates.

9

1.1.3 - Table 3 - All are State of rule in Mercosur

ARGENTINA	Article 27.- The federal Government is obliged to strengthen its relations of peace and trade with foreign powers through treaties that are in conformity with the principles of public law established in this Constitution.
BRASIL	Article 1 The Federative Republic of Brazil, formed by the interrelated union of the States and Municipalities and the Federal District, is a Democratic State of Law and has as its foundation:
PARAGUAI	Article 1 - IN THE FORM OF STATE AND GOVERNMENT The Republic of Paraguay is forever free and independent. It is constituted as a Social State of law, unitary, indivisible, and decentralized in the manner established by this Constitution and laws.
URUGUAI	Article 4. - Sovereignty in all its fullness exists radically in the Nation, which has the exclusive right to establish its laws, in the way that will be expressed later.
VENEZUELA	Article 2. Venezuela is constituted as a democratic and social State of Law and Justice, which advocates as higher values of its legal system and its action, life, liberty, justice, equality, solidarity, democracy, social responsibility and in general, the pre-eminence of human rights, ethics and political pluralism.

There is no doubt that all MERCOSUR member countries are constituted with a republican form, a representative system and a democratic regime of government. We are not republics of medicine, geography or philosophy, but of law.

This means that the constituent power, that from which comes the whole power of the Nation, has in theory created representatively democratic Republics and whose destinies are in the hands of political and juridical spheres that really feel they have the duty to represent the aspirations of the Mercosur members.

The question that the political-juridical classes of Mercosur must ask on a daily basis is what do the people want? Our comparative study shows that the answer is objectively found in all Constitutions of the member countries of Mercosur, insofar as they promise housing, health, education, work, security and leisure.

Thus, having proved sufficient constitutional symmetry, we can go beyond the economic integration that is still happening in some fields, such as the legal prediction of the Brazilian government on the preference margins in the acquisition of products for the Public Administration, as extracted from art. 3 of Law No. 8,666 / 1993, Law of Bidd, as follows:

"Art. 3. The bid is intended to ensure compliance with the constitutional principle of isonomy, selection of the most advantageous proposal for the administration and promotion of sustainable national development and will be processed and judged in strict accordance with the basic principles of legality, impersonality, morality, equality, publicity, administrative probity, attachment to the convening instrument, the objective judgment and those related to it. (Drafting provided by Law No. 12.349, of 2010)

Paragraph 1 - It is prohibited for public agents:

I - To admit, predict, include or tolerate, in acts of convocation, clauses or conditions that compromise, restrict or frustrate their competitive character, including in the case of cooperative societies, and establish preferences or distinctions due to naturalness, of the headquarters or domicile of the bidders or of any other circumstance that is irrelevant or irrelevant to the specific object of the contract, except as provided in §§5o to 12th of this article. (Drafting provided by Law No. 12,349, of 2010)

II - To establish differentiated treatment of commercial, legal, labor, social security or any other nature, between Brazilian and foreign companies, including with regard to currency, modality and place of payment, even when involving international agencies, except as provided in the following paragraph and in art. 3 of Law no. 8,248, of October 23, 1991.

Paragraph 2. In equal conditions, as a tie-breaking criterion, preference shall be given successively to goods and services:

I - (Revoked by Law No. 12,349, of 2010)

II - Produced in the country;

III - Produced or rendered by Brazilian companies.

IV - Produced or rendered by companies that invest in research and technology development in the Country. (Included by Law no. 11,196, of 2005)

(...)

Paragraph 5. In the bidding processes set forth in the caput, a margin of preference may be established for manufactured products and for national services that comply with Brazilian technical standards. (Included by Law no. 12,349, of 2010)

Paragaph 6 The margin of preference referred to in § 5 shall be established on the basis of studies reviewed periodically, within a period not exceeding five (5) years, taking into account: (Included in Law 12499 of 2010)

I - Employment and income generation; (Included by Law no. 12,349, of 2010) II - effect on the collection of federal, state and municipal taxes; (Included by Law no. 12,349, of 2010)

III - Development and technological innovation in the country; (Included by Law no. 12,349, of 2010)

IV - Additional cost of products and services; and (Included by Law No. 12,349 of 2010)

V - In its reviews, retrospective analysis of results. (Included in Law No. 12,349 of 2010)

Paragraph 7 for manufactured products and national services resulting from technological development and innovation in the country, a margin of preference may be established in addition to that provided for in Paragraph 5. (Included by Law no. 12,349, of 2010)

(...)

Paragraph 9 The provisions contained in paragraphs 5 and 7 of this article do not apply to goods and services whose production capacity or service in the country is lower: (Included by Law 12349 of 2010)

I - The quantity to be acquired or contracted; or (Included by Law No. 12,349 of 2010)

II - To the amount established pursuant to § 7 of art. 23 of this Law, when applicable. (Included by Law no. 12,349, of 2010)

Paragfraph 10. The margin of preference referred to in § 5 may be extended, wholly or in part, to goods and services originating in the States Parties to the Southern Common Market (MERCOSUR). (Included by Law no. 12.349, of 2010)"

The transcribed text shows that the principle of equality is relevant to the law, but also demonstrates that the law can establish privileges when such differentiations objectify the balance, as it appears from subsection II of article 3 retrotranscript.

Based on the legislative symmetry of the Mercosur member countries, there is no doubt about the possibility of unifying criminal, procedural penal and administrative-disciplinary legislation dealing with crimes and acts of improbity against the Mercosur Public Administrations, by creating a permanent Court of Justice with jurisdiction to prosecute and judge the offenses, whose scope extends to more than one country in the Mercosur community.

The democracy, as a form of government is enshrined in all the constitutions of the Mercosur through:

1– Universal suffrage; and
2– Direct and secret vote in which the people elect representatives to express their political-juridical will.

Based on the symmetry of the constitutions of Mercosur member countries, we feel safe to make our own, the words of Professor La Palombara (1982: 19) when he says:

> "Social sciences, including political science, are today, more than in the past, capable of understanding, explaining, and perhaps predicting the behavior of men and organizations.

> (...)

> "More than two thousand years ago, Aristotle and his disciples studied the constitutions of 158 city-states, hoping to illuminate the way for the ideal polis. As every newspaper reveals, more or less twenty centuries of experience do not give us much proof that we are on the right path (...) This confidence stems from the certainty that the social sciences, including political science, are today, more than in the past, able to understand, explain, and perhaps predict the behavior of men and organizations."

CHAPTER 2

Hierarchy of International Treaties in The Constitutions of Mercosur

An integration or unification of legislation between States must be dealt with in the framework of Public International Law.

Júlio Barboza (2003: 107) writes that Treaties and Agreements exist as a manifestation of the will of the subjects of International Law and exist to create, modify or extinguish rights:

> "Treaties are usually defined as agreements of wills between subjects of International Law, aimed at creating, modifying or extinguishing international obligations. There are several denominations to designate this: Conventions, agreements, protocols, agreements, etc. "Conventions" or "conventions" usually apply to multilateral instruments or codifiers ("Convention on the protection of biological diversity", "Vienna Convention on diplomatic relations", etc.). "Charter" or "pacts" designated the constitutional instruments of international organizations) Charter of the United Nations, Covenant of the League of Nations). "Protocols" are usually instruments that serve as corollaries to others (Montreal Protocol within the framework of the Vienna Convention on the Protection of the Ozone Layer). Other treaty names may be given: "commitment", "modus vivendi", "concordat" - if the Church is part "statute", etc.,

but its general denomination is that of treaties and all respond to the concept given above.

Therefore, the appropriate norm to promote unification is an open and multilateral Convention among the member states of Mercosur.

It should be open to allow the subsequent adherence of those who did not take part in the various stages of celebration, such as text elaboration, negotiation, adoption of text, authentication of text, manifestation of multilateral consent, signature, ratification, as the following Articles:

„PART VIII

FINAL PROVISIONS

Article 81

Signature

The present Convention shall be open for signature by all Member States of the United Nations or of any of the specialized agencies or the International Atomic Energy Agency, as well as by all parties to the Statute of the International Court of Justice and any other Invited by the General Assembly of the United Nations to become a party to the Convention as follows: until 30 November 1969 at the Federal Ministry of Foreign Affairs of the Republic of Austria and thereafter until 30 April 1970, at the United Nations Headquarters in New York.

Article 82 Ratio
This Convention shall be subject to ratification. The instruments of ratification shall be deposited with the Secretary-General of the United Nations.

Article 83

Membership

> This Convention shall remain open for accession by any State belonging to any of the categories referred to in article 81. The instruments of accession shall be deposited with the Secretary-General of the United Nations."

Certainly, a Convention on the unification of criminal, procedural penal and administrative-disciplinary legislation, with the creation of a Permanent Criminal Court with criminal and administrative jurisdiction, will not have the nature of a Treaty of contract but of a "Normative Treaty". Here is how Júlio Barboza (2003: 111) differentiates one from another:

> "They differ in that the former express a will of a part that is different and complementary to the will of the other (a party wants to buy and the other sell) and the latter translate a common will, which is expressed in rules general, as in the United Nations Convention on the Law of the Sea... "

The Vienna Convention is the law of treaties. Their considerations, findings, historical memories and beliefs clearly indicate how international law can contribute to building the ideals of democratic states of law.

The Brazilian government by the Decree 7,030 / 2009, enacts the Vienna Convention on the Law of Treaties, concluded on May 23, 1969, with important considerations on the importance of the International Law to keep peace and help in the worlds development. Here is the transcription of an excerpt with such characteristics:

> "Considering the fundamental role of treaties in the history of international relations,
>
> Recognizing the increasing importance of treaties as a source of international law and as a means of developing peaceful cooperation among nations, whatever their constitutional and social systems may be,

Noting that the principles of free consent and good faith and the pacta sunt servanda rule are universally recognized,

Affirming that disputes relating to treaties, such as other international disputes, must be settled by peaceful means and in accordance with the principles of Justice and International Law,

Recalling the determination of the peoples of the United Nations to create the necessary conditions for the maintenance of justice and respect for the obligations arising from the treaties,

Aware of the principles of international law embodied in the Charter of the United Nations, such as the principles of equal rights and self-determination of peoples, the sovereign equality and independence of all States, non-intervention in the internal affairs of States, the prohibition of the threat or use of force and universal respect and observance of human rights and fundamental freedoms for all,

Believing that the codification and progressive development of the law of treaties reached in this Convention will promote the purposes of the United Nations enunciated in the Charter, which are the maintenance of international peace and security, the development of friendly relations and the achieving cooperation among nations,

Affirming that the rules of customary international law shall continue to govern matters not regulated by the provisions of this Convention."

Concerning the Treaties as means and resources for the materialization of individual and collective rights and guarantees that create substantial democracies, the text of Decree 7,030 / 2009 that enacts the Convention declares:

"SECTION 4

Treaties and Third Parties

Article 34

General Rule Relating to Third States
A treaty does not create obligations or rights for a third State without its consent.

Article 35

Treaties Establishing Obligations for Third States
An obligation arises for a third State from a treaty provision if the parties to the treaty intend to create the obligation under that provision and the third State expressly accepts in writing that obligation.

Article 36

Treaties Creating Rights for Third States

1. A right arises for a third State from a treaty provision if the parties to the treaty intend to confer by virtue of that provision such a right either to a third State or to a group of States to which belongs to all States and the third State therein. Their consent shall be presumed unless otherwise indicated, unless the treaty provides otherwise.

2. A State exercising a right under paragraph 1 shall, for the exercise of that right, respect the conditions laid down in the treaty or established in accordance with the treaty.

Article 37

Revocation or Modification of Obligations or Rights of Third States

1. Any obligation arising in respect of a third State under article 35 may only be revoked or withdrawn with the consent of the parties to the treaty and of the third State, unless it is established that they have otherwise agreed.

2. Any right which has arisen for a third State under article 36 may not be revoked or modified by the parties, if it has been established that the law was not revocable or subject to change without the consent of the third State.

Article 38

Rules of a Treaty Made Mandatory for Third States by

International Costume

Nothing in Articles 34 to 37 prevents a treaty rule from becoming binding upon third States as a customary rule of international law recognized as such."

As the focus of this chapter is not "Treaty" but its hierarchy in the internal legal systems, we present in the table that follows the comparative study that we carried out in the constitutions of Mercosur member countries:

2.1 Table: The hierarchy of the treaties in Constitutions of Mercosur

ARGENTINA	Article 31.- This Constitution, the laws of the Nation that, as a consequence, are dictated by Congress and treaties with foreign powers are the supreme law of the Nation; and the authorities of each province are obliged to conform to them, notwithstanding any provision to the contrary contained in the laws or provincial constitutions, except for the province of Buenos Aires, the treaties ratified after the Pact of November 11, 1859.

BRAZIL	Art. 5 All are equal before the law, without distinction of any kind, guaranteeing to Brazilians and foreigners residing in the country the inviolability of the right to life, liberty, equality, security and property, under the terms following: (...) Paragraph 2 - The rights and guarantees expressed in this Constitution do not exclude others arising from the regime and the principles adopted by it, or international treaties to which the Federative Republic of Brazil is a party. Paragraph 3 International treaties and conventions on human rights that are approved in each House of the National Congress in two rounds, for three fifths of the votes of the respective members, shall be equivalent to the constitutional amendments. (Included by Constitutional Amendment no. 45, 2004) (Legislative Decree with force of Constitutional Amendment) § 4 Brazil submits to the jurisdiction of the International Criminal Court whose creation has manifested its adhesion. (Incorporated by Constitutional Amendment No. 45, 2004)
PARAGUAI	Article 137 - OF THE SUPREMACY OF THE CONSTITUTION The supreme law of the Republic is the Constitution. This, the treaties, conventions and international agreements approved and ratified, the laws passed by Congress and other legal provisions of lower rank, sanctioned in consequence, integrate the positive national law in the order of priority stated. (...) Article 141 - INTERNATIONAL TREATIES Validly concluded international treaties, approved by congressional law, and whose instruments of ratification are exchanged or deposited, form part of the internal legal order with the hierarchy determined in Article 137.

URUGUAI	Article 6.- In the international treaties that the Republic holds, it will propose the clause that all differences that arise between the contracting parties will be decided by arbitration or other peaceful means. The Republic will seek the social and economic integration of the Latin American States, especially as regards the common defense of their products and raw materials. Likewise, it will tend to the effective complementation of its public services. (...) Article 239.- The Supreme Court of Justice is responsible for: 1o) Judging all offenders of the Constitution, without exception; on crimes against the Right of People and Admiralty Causes; in matters relating to treaties, pacts and conventions with other States; know in the cases of diplomats accredited in the Republic, in the cases provided by International Law.
VENEZUELA	Article 23. The treaties, pacts and conventions related to human rights, signed and ratified by Venezuela, have a constitutional hierarchy and prevail in the internal order, to the extent that they contain rules on their enjoyment and exercise more favorable to those established by this Constitution and the law of the Republic, and are of immediate and direct application by the courts and other organs of the Public Power.

The Supreme Courts of Mercosur have discussed the hierarchy of Treaties, the applicability of their provisions in time and space, as well as the possibility of creating a criminal court as supranational justice.

Here are excerpts from these dialogues between the Mercosur Supreme Courts (2007: 49-61, 153-175) which, given the historical-juridical value we deem primordial for those who wish to understand the subject in depth, in the quotations, convinced that the one who loves knowledge never sees the effort of learning as a loss of time:

"Being admitted the transfer of competences, this would
solve in advance an issue of significant importance:

the incorporation of the regulations resulting from the integration process. In effect, given the delegation of state powers, the organs of integration will have the capacity to issue legal norms, which will not need specific internalization in the internal law of the Member States. Otherwise, as in Mercosur, there will be, in addition to the right of integration, so many parallel rights - with the same content - as States Parties to the system (eg "Mercosur law", "Argentine law", "Brazilian law"). "," Paraguayan law "and" Uruguayan law ").

Dr. Maristela Basso, Professor at the University of San Pablo, stressed the importance of art. 4th, single paragraph, of the Brazilian Federal Constitution of 1988, for the integration of Brazil in Mercosur, highlighting that this provision makes up the chapter of the Magna Carta dedicated to the fundamental principles of domestic law. Another constitutional rule that deserved consideration was the art. 5th, §2, around which three doctrinal positions on the relationship between treaties and domestic laws have been elaborated, ranging from the irrelevance of inclusion in the CF 1988, to the idea that such article prescribes superiority of treaties on national laws.

He added that the jurisprudence of the Supreme Court of Argentina, in supporting the doctrine of the superiority of international treaties over laws, perceived that the opposite position would violate the separation of the Powers of the State, by virtue of an act of Congress incompatible with a treaty. This question has been variable in the jurisprudence of the Federal Supreme Court - STF.

In a first stage, the Court defended the understanding according to which the treaties were hierarchically superior to the laws of the state, while in a second orientation (initiated with the Extraordinary Resource 80.004), the doctrine of the STF changed radically, considering that both types of standards, treaties and laws, are in the same normative plane, prevailing in case of conflict the most recent.

He recalled that the STF had no opportunity, since the 1970s, to speak out again on the question of the relationship between international law and domestic law. This latest trend of the Brazilian high court, understandable in the context of the 70s, seems hardly sustainable at present, considering the new world scenario and the theories in vogue in the doctrine. In this regard, he advocated the early ratification of the Vienna Convention on the law of treaties by the Brazilian government. The inconvenience of this position becomes even more controversial when it comes to Mercosur. Finally, he stressed that Brazil must define itself, making the option "Mercosur si" or "Mercosur no".

(...)

Mr. Nelson Jobim: (...) The experience I had with the National Congress shows that the problem in Brazil, as far as the hierarchy of treaties is concerned, is inextricably linked to the question of the manifestation of the international will of the Parents. In our system, perhaps similar to some of you, the treaty is managed, exclusively as it could not be, with the Executive Branch. And in taking or being sent treaties, signed by the Executive Power, to the National Congress, can not amend the treaties, because the international will of the country manifested itself directly at the international negotiating table. With this circumstance, there is an exclusion of the Brazilian Legislative Branch in the manifestation of the international will of the Country. Hence why Congress reacts to any kind of treaty prevalence to ordinary law, since in ordinary law it, National Congress, have absolute participation, whereas in the treaty it is relatively excluded.

This is the great political problem in Brazil. I remember that in 1989 one of the greatest ambassadors

I had ever met in Brazil, Ambassador Paulo Nogueira Batista, when he had seen Dr. Ulisses Guimarães as Chairman of the Committee on Foreign Relations of the Chamber of Deputies, had suggested a formula for that There could be a permeability in the sense of the participation of this Commission itself in the discussion of the manifestation of the will. I believe that if Brazil does not solve the problem of the Executive-Legislative relationship in the formation of The National Congress will almost certainly give up spaces, because it would be to grant powers to the Executive, independently of the more substantial participation of the Legislative Power in this matter, the political question.

In 1993, at the time of the constitutional revision, I proposed that texts produced by international organizations in which Brazil adhered to a treaty should have their internal validity in Brazil, regardless of the participation of the National Congress. And the Congress reviewed, at that time, rejecting, since I got only sixty votes of the four hundred required votes.

Professor Roberto Ruiz Díaz Labrano (Paraguay): The first thing I thought of the other exhibitions was the fact that there is clearly a perception of a constitutional obstacle to the progress of integration.

There is a perception that some Constitutions need to be reformed or need some adjustments. It has been said that the main obstacle to evolving and overcoming the problem, which means this issue of hierarchy in the application of treaties to laws in the Brazilian constitutional legal order, is due to political issue, an appreciation that I think it is important to take note of these meetings. (...)

Another important issue already mentioned is that the order of constitutional normative interpretation has two priority approaches:

1) The later rule repeals the previous one. Applied to the Constitution in the Brazilian legal order, we would have a law of the Legislative Power could eventually repeal an international treaty.

2) The special law prevails over the law of a general nature. There we find again a sustenance for the prevalence of the legal order that emanates from the treaties in front of the national laws, because the treaties have a content of special nature. They are linked to specific international relations. They are linked to aspects contained in a treaty where the relationship is clearly specific. What national law could, without also affecting the constitutional order, be introduced in this aspect of international relations?

I am certainly talking about the Brazilian constitutional order, but I am doing a purely interpretative aspect. What we want to say is that an international treaty obeys a special category and nature. It prevails over any general norm and it is difficult for it to find, in an internal norm, the equivalent or an internal norm that refers to the special aspects of which international law is concerned. (...)

Another element that also appears to support the existence of a supranational legal system is that of integration.

The integration that appears in the Constitutions of the four States in a different way. It is remarkable the difference that exists and we must highlight the difference that exists between the way in which this aspect conceives the Argentine Constitution, which refers to supra-state bodies. The Paraguayan Constitution refers to supra-state legal systems. The Argentine Constitution is therefore part of the creation of the body that will create that legal order hierarchically superior to the internal order. The Paraguayan Constitution starts from the recognition that as a State it necessarily recognizes existence - because it participates in an international community in order of equality with other States in its international action - it recognizes a supranational legal order from the creation of organs or from the possibility of creation.

We do not see a substantial obstacle in the Uruguayan Constitution and in the Brazilian Constitution, if a clearly political obstacle and political will must be harmonized and must be understood because if we do not understand that reality, we will hardly be able to overcome this so-called "obstacle" that maybe, perhaps, it is preventing the region from adapting to the time the region needs for its international relationship.

Mr. Leslie Van Rompaey Servillo, President of the Supreme Court of Uruguay: Thank you. Buenos dias.

a) Statement of the Problem

In the approach to this problem, we start from the premise that Mercosur is currently an intergovernmental process by decision of the States Parties. If these resolve to take a step forward in the integration process, then the problem will arise for the legal evolution of Mercosur, which is constituted by the constitutional asymmetries of the States Parties when it comes to enabling the direct application of community law or creation. of supranational bodies.

At the risk of being repetitive, we know that the Argentine Constitution is the clearest from the 1994 reform (Article 75 paragraph 24) authorizing the "delegation of powers and jurisdiction to suprastate organizations in conditions of reciprocity and equality."

It is also favorable to supranationality the Constitution of Paraguay, whose article 145, "admits a supranational legal order."

The constitutional texts of the Eastern Republic of Uruguay (Article 6, paragraph 2) and of the Federative Republic of Brazil (Article 4) show generic and programmatic statements, but in my view, in no way, at least in the case of Uruguay, hinder the development of the integration process. (...)

Thus, from a first observation of the situation in each of the four member countries of Mercosur, an apparent situation of disharmony arose between the constitutional regimes of each one of them. Indeed, it is feasible to make a classification that includes two groups. The first one, composed of Argentina and Paraguay, which includes in its fundamental laws the supremacy of treaties over national laws, on the one hand, and, on the other, special provisions in order to facilitate regional integration processes.

The respective regime of both countries exhibits practically the same modalities.

The second group of states would be made up of Brazil and Uruguay, countries whose Magna Carta does not foresee the aforementioned constitutional system, at least not expressly, for its two Mercosur partners.

Article 4 of the Brazilian Constitution states that "The Federative Republic of Brazil will seek the economic, political, social and cultural integration of the peoples of Latin America, approving the formation of a Latin American Community of Nations."

The Constitution, however, does not foresee explicit rules on integration that facilitate this type of process, either by modifying the order of priority of its internal norms, giving the possibility to internal organs to delegate faculties in a regional order or establishing a procedure that alleviates the incorporation of the rules that derive from the decisions taken by a regional structure.

In the case of Uruguay, the constitutional norms that refer to the subject are Article 6, paragraph 2, which states that: "The Republic shall seek the social and economic integration of the States.

Latin Americans, especially as regards the common defense of their products and raw materials. Likewise, it will tend to the effective complementation of its public services. "(...)

b) Apparent asymmetry with respect to the Constitutions of Brazil and Uruguay

In Paraguay and Argentina, the national Constitutions establish the supremacy of international treaties over domestic law. In Brazil, or at least in my opinion, clearly in Uruguay, it would seem that the effects of the former could be modified as a consequence of the enactment of national laws. According to this vision, as long as there is no convergence of constitutional principles, it would be very difficult to advance in the integration process and, especially, in the process of "aggregation of sovereignties".

Underlining a constitutional obstacle sounds intimidating: if it is about doing something as fundamental as reforming a constitutional norm, the political magnitude of the challenge appears immeasurable. I would like to emphasize that in Uruguay the successive constitutional reforms have always been linked to issues of an electoral nature or to urgent political needs of the administration and government of the State. It would be very difficult to achieve a constitutional reform specifically aimed at the possibility of creating supranational bodies by direct application of the regulations of the community organizations. (BRAZIL, Supreme Federal Court, Supreme Court Meetings: Challenges and Prospects, Mercosul Integration Process, Brasília: Forum of Supreme Courts, 2007. pp. 56-58.)

The Monist thesis and integration

The Monist thesis - consecrated in most of Latin America - presupposes the existence of a universal legal system, international law, to which national rights must be subordinated and maintains that internal and international norms form a single integrated legal order and that when a State adopts the contents of a Treaty, it is duly incorporated into the national legal order without the need for transformation.

The different processes have led from the state structures to a favorable tendency to integrate them into wide continental spaces. This phenomenon has brought with it a weakening of the traditional notion of sovereignty, since integration from the perspective of law necessarily involves the delegation of national powers in favor of supra-state areas.

The contribution of jurisprudence

Jurisprudence, on the other hand, also underwent an important evolution.

In 1992, the jurisprudence of the Supreme Court of Argentina decides the primacy of the treaties over the laws of internal law. It was the famous Ekmekdjian c / Sofovich ruling today.

The supreme court held "that (...) the violation of an international treaty can occur both by the establishment of internal rules that prescribe a manifestly contrary conduct, and by the failure to establish provisions that make it possible to comply. Both situations would be contradictory with the previous international ratification of the treaty; in other words, they would mean the breach or rejection of the treaty, with the harmful consequences that could derive from it ". He then expresses "that the

Vienna Convention on the law of treaties with primacy to conventional international law over domestic law (...)

This Convention has altered the situation of the legal systems of the countries that ratify it, because the legal proposal according to which there is no normative basis to accord priority to the treaty before the law is no longer accurate. Such normative foundation lies in the art. 27 of the Vienna Convention (...) "Then it is manifest" that the necessary application of art. 27 of the Vienna Convention requires the organs of the ratifying States to assign primacy to the treaty in the event of con fl ict with any contrary domestic norm or the failure to enact provisions that, in their effects, amount to a breach of the international treaty on the terms of the aforementioned art. 27. "After the previous one at the level of the Supreme Court of Argentina, three new sentences are issued, which only confirm the change. These are the cases "Fibraca Constructora (...)", "Hagelin (...)" and "Cafés La Virginia S.A."

e) Solution to the Problem

This evolution in the world in terms of integration in large economic spaces is the phenomenon that Capeletti has considered as the "transnational dimension of law and justice".

In international law today, the value of the primacy of the international order over the interna- tional is value, which is why it is inappropriate to invoke internal norms as a justification for the breach of international obligations (Articles 26 and 27 of the Convention) of Vienna on the Law of Treaties). In a way, the constitutional norms that many countries (Argentina, Chile, Paraguay, Colombia, etc.) recognize expressly the supralegality and / or constitutionality of the treaties, are part of this line.

The constitutions that do not foresee this system like the Brazilian and the Uruguayan do it through the ratification of the Vienna Convention on the Law of Treaties; this criterion, which in principle refers only to ratified treaties, is accentuated in the field of human rights, in respect of which the effectiveness of specific international instruments is even sustained regardless of their ratification. There are obvious examples: the Universal Declaration of Human Rights of the UN of 1948, the American Declaration of Rights and Duties of Man of the same year.

The treaties are a source of International Law according to the provisions of art. 38 of the Statute of the International Court of Justice and therefore must be respected by ratifying countries regardless of their constitutional regimes.

Both Brazil and Uruguay have ratified the Treaty of Asuncion, constituent of the Mercosur, and the Vienna Convention on the Law of Treaties (it was ratified by Uruguay and in the international scope in a large part of its rules can be used as customary law).

This last Convention provides in its preamble that the principles of free consent and good faith and the norm "pacta sunt servanda" are universally recognized.

Its articles 26 and 27 provide that any treaty in force binds the parties and must be complied with by them in good faith, and that a State party to a treaty may not invoke the provisions of its domestic law as a justification for breach of the Treaty.

These rules clearly mark the principle of the "irreversibility of Community commitments" which means that there is no legal return to the Community. It is not allowed to question the commitments once assumed;

it is not allowed to nationalize again the sectors that have already passed under the authority of the Community.

It is at the moment of preparing to ratify the treaties when each State has had or should consider and solve the constitutional problems that are posed to it. Each one owns the solution that he gives them; but once an international commitment has been accepted with all freedom, there is here a historical fact about which it is no longer possible to return.

It is against the good faith of international treaties that a member state or one of its authorities, for example a jurisdiction, tried to question the accepted commitments by invoking, "a posteriori", constitutional obstacles.

Therefore, after the international instrument has been ratified by the States, there is a supranational and supra-constitutional legal order that must also be applied internally by the judges and other national organs of the State.

From what we understand, both in the case of Brazil and Uruguay - we already saw that Argentina and Paraguay have already solved the problem in their own constitutional texts - it is not necessary to reform their Constitutions but to apply the Treaty of Asunción and in consistent with it, harmonize the interpretation and application of the rest of their respective internal rights in line with what is provided by international regulations and modern jurisprudence and doctrine in this regard. (...)

3 ° MEETING OF SUPREME COURTS OF TWO STATES-PARTIES

Mr. Nelson Jobim: We live a fundamental question in Brazil, that is, we do not yet have, Mr. President of the National Congress, an option in the sense of the prevalence of community law. Community law in Brazil, that is to say, the law of treaties, in Brazil, as you all know, is an identical right, absolutely identical to the ordinary law. so much so that a treaty signed by Brazil, of any nature, whether bilaterally or multilaterally, by our constitutional system, is susceptible of derogation or even of revocation by simple ordinary law, voted in the National Congress, even of initiative (...)

Please remind us that we have a historical problem: Brazil, for reasons of national unity policy, especially since the Empire, has always turned its back on Hispanic America. This, in Brazilian memory, was suffocated both in the Empire period and in the First Republic, because it was understood that the studies of Hispanic America or the permeability with it could lead to the disunity of Portuguese America. It was, therefore, a condition for the maintenance of the National Territory and the unity of Portuguese America to forget about Hispanic America. There was no study of the history of Hispanic America in Brazil. The most that there were were the disputes of Brazil, via Rio Grande do Sul, with Argentina and Uruguay. The speech always about the possibility of either the Argentines, the Castilians of the eastern band, or of Oribe or Rosas, enter by Rio Grande. This story was radical in the head of all of us.

It was not until the second half of the twentieth century that Brazil began to turn its eyes to Hispanic America. For us, the study of Europe was more important than studies with Argentina. The issues between the Unitarians and the Federais in Argentina for us were completely strange and utterly uninteresting. We looked at the eastern band with a certain contempt, as if it had been an English historical construction to try to obstruct the pretensions of the Brazilian Empire.

The signing by the judiciary of the Charter of Brasilia in 2004 reveals the institutional improvement of our

34

economic bloc. This bloc represents the very clear option in favor of political stability, social justice and economic prosperity beyond national boundaries. On the basis of this historical construction are increased judicial co-operation, and the further development of the system of dispute settlement. (...)

What are we today?

Because sometimes you lose track of what we are. We constitute the largest integrated space on the planet, the first data that astonishes those who are not warned. Seventeen million three hundred thousand square kilometers are the ten South American countries, three hundred and eighty million inhabitants, energy reserves for one hundred years, the three great rivers, the Orinoco, the Amazon, the Paraná and the Río de la Plata, are the three unparalleled water basins. Our mountain ranges treasure very important minerals, fertilize our lands, produce food in proportions that also amaze and sometimes you get angry when you see that South Americans without understanding the problem and say: why are we discussing the FTAA issue with the United States? Why did a man say, days gone by, do not we get angry with Japan that has higher subsidies? And what does that have to do? If we are not competitors of Japan. And the European Union also has high subsidies and we are not competitors of the EU, only one data, only one and everything is clarified.

The Mercosur produces forty-eight percent to put a product of the leaves that are produced at a planetary level, data from FAO last year. Forty-eight percent. United States, thirty-five percent. They are our competitors. And prices are depressed by subsidies for production and also for the export of those products. And they tell us that commerce is free, how free? Is that there is free trade for what suits them and free trade for what does not suit them, where we have really competitive advantages, there is no longer free, with

35

an argument that can not be discussed. And our Congress is very protectionist, they tell us from the north. They blame Congress and it's true. But the truth is that we do not have an ideological problem, it's a commercial problem, that's why this issue of Alca, yes, Alca, does not have to do with this process of ours. Our process is an integration process that has as a mirror the European Union. It is a different thing, there is no incompatibility in having an integration process and having free trade with all countries or regions of the world that suits us, because it is a commercial issue of convenience. We do not go where it does not suit us. (...)

In sum, notwithstanding the merit that should be recognized by the ECJ, his work is not the result of a solitary effort, but of the context formed by a kind of community of legal thought that, in a certain way, both preceded his doctrine and accompanied it.

And if this is the case, it is worth asking today if there is a legally homogeneous legal community in the Mercosur to hegemonize another interpretive community and, in any case, what we are doing about it.

But I want to insist on the two initial points of my speech, the necessity of superiority over the treaty of national laws and the binding nature of the decisions of the permanent review court, only in this way can I achieve the ideal that I aspire to, that national judges become community judges. (...)

Minister Antonio Fretes, President of the Supreme Court of Justina of Paraguay:

The right of integration, in its most advanced development, such as community law, requires due attention because it is the manifestation in the institutional legal will of States that have decided to build a legal community through integration.

(...) In the integration processes, such as the European one, it was the jurisdictional bodies that interpreted and applied the community law, through the national bodies in the first place, and then through the Court of Justice of the Communities The European bodies, as the ultimate body on community law, have contributed to the credibility of the integration process and have made legal security effective.

It has been the Community judicial body that has sided with the legal nature of the European process through the already classic issues "Van Gend & Loos" and "Costa / Enel". 1 In the first of these classic issues, the European Court exposed:

(...) The objective of the EEC Treaty, which is to establish a common market whose operation directly affects the people of the Community, implies that the Treaty constitutes something more than an Agreement, which only creates reciprocal obligations between the Contracting States (...) this conception is confirmed in the Preamble of the Treaty, which, in addition to the Governments, refers to the peoples, and does so, in a more concrete way, through the creation of bodies in which sovereign powers are institutionalized (...) affects both the Member States and their citizens (...) for these reasons, it must be concluded that the Community constitutes a new legal order of international law, in favor of which the Member States have limited their sovereignty, although in a restricted area, and whose subjects are not only the Member States, but also their nationals. (...)

PANEL I - APPLICATION OF MERCOSUR STANDARDS IN THE PARTIES

Enrique Santiago Petracchi, President of the Supreme Court of Justice of Argentina: Because it is an intergovernmental model, Mercosur in its original design lacks supranational bodies. Consequently, any delegation of legislative or jurisdictional powers is absent, with the effects that derive from it when applying the right that emanates from the bodies with decision-making powers.

The legal system applicable to possible conflicts in the area is notoriously different from the so-called "Community Law" developed in the framework of the model of paradigmatic integration of the 20th century, the European Community. Among the greatest asymmetries, it should be noted that European community standards have a hierarchy superior to those of the entire domestic legal system, enjoy direct effect and are of immediate application. These principles were bypassing the interpretation made by the Court of Justice of the European Communities and laid the foundations on which its legal system was built.

The Mercosur, on the other hand, still does not possess the organic and normative characteristics of this block, so that its rules, when they are applied, are subject to a plurality of interpretations that depend on the jurisdictions that operate with these legal sources.

The direct effect of the rules, which reinforces the effectiveness of Community Law, gives individuals the possibility of invoking them before their respective national jurisdictions, requiring the application of treaties, regulations, directives or community decisions, which matters the obligation for the judge to make use of these texts, whatever the legislation of the country to which it belongs. For this the norm must be clear and precise, complete, sufficient to itself, and the rule must be unconditional, not subject to any term or reservation.

When ruling on case 26/1962, the aforementioned Court of Justice pointed out that the Community constitutes a new legal ordinance of international law, in benefit of which, the States have limited, even in restricted matters, their sovereign rights., and whose subjects are not only the Member States but also their nationals. Community law, independent of the legislation of the Member States, as well as creating obligations for individuals, is also intended to engender rights that are found in its legal assets. The Court thus shows the supranational character of Community law.

Confronted with a possible conflict between Community law and national law, the local judge resorts to the procedure for the submission of preliminary rulings before that Court, in order to ensure the uniform interpretation of Community law in all Member States. Inspired by the mechanisms of referral to the constitutional courts regulated by the German Basic Law and the Italian Constitution, the centralized interpretation ensures uniformity.

The duty to ensure that every directly applicable community norm is respected in the member states derives from the power of national jurisdictions to decide on the application of Community law, which is why the national judge is, strictly speaking, the first community judge. (...)

Just a few words about the Argentine Constitution, since the constitutional asymmetries have already been addressed in the previous Meeting. But I think it is of interest to recall the distinction incorporated in 1994 to the text of the Basic Law of my country with regard to international agreements. As a general principle, the superiority of all international treaties in force for the Republic with respect to national and provincial laws2 was established (art.75 inc. 22 C.N.). Likewise, a series of treaties on human rights, expressly mentioned, reached the constitutional hierarchy, while a regime was envisaged that makes it possible to incorporate, with equal hierarchy, other conventions related to that matter.

In line with what I have just indicated, but with more emphasis if it is Mercosur, it is worth remembering the new art. 75 paragraph 244 of the Constitution, since it expressly enables the approval of integration treaties that delegate powers and jurisdiction to supra-state organizations, or that, as this norm indicates, in conditions of reciprocity and equality, and as long as they respect the democratic order and human rights. Moreover, the constitutional precept, foreseeably, provides that the rules issued as a consequence of said integration agreements will have a higher hierarchy than the laws. (...)

In the Mercosur field, and even when the Decisions, Resolutions and Directives issued by the respective bodies are obligatory for the States Parties, due to the nature of "legal sources of Mercosur", as was clarified in the Protocol of Ouro Preto, the functions of the Common Market Council, the Common Market Group and the Trade Commission are substantially oriented to trade and customs policies and do not include the issuance of norms directly applicable in the member states. However, the normative hierarchy is contemplated in art. 19 of the Protocol of Brasilia to say that the Arbitral Tribunal will decide the dispute on the basis of the provisions of the Treaty of Asunción, of the agreements concluded in the framework of the same, of the Decisions of the Common Market Council, of the Resolutions of the Market Group Common, as well as the principles and provisions of international law applicable in the matter. The Protocol of Ouro Preto adds the Directives of the Trade Commission, in its art. 43

The methodology for the adoption of the referred standards is by consensus, and its obligation would imply that once they have been issued, the States Parties are responsible for their internalization and compliance. And on this aspect, that of compliance, we must bear in mind the provisions of the aforementioned Vienna Convention on the Law of Treaties (article 27), and the principles of good faith and of pacta sunt servando of wide-ranging custom.

Despite its vocation of obligation, these rules do not, as mentioned, have an immediate, direct and prevalent application, despite the aforementioned commitment to adopt the necessary measures to ensure compliance in the respective territories. It was already specified in the II Encuentro, according to the data provided by the Technical Secretariat, that only 50% of the rules issued by the decision-making bodies had been incorporated into the internal legal order of the countries.

Auspiciously, the latest reports on the degree of validity of Mercosur standards in the States Parties indicate that of the 1596 norms approved between 1991 and December 2004 - Common Market Decisions, Common Market Group Resolutions and Commission Directives Trade -, 68% of them are valid in the four States.

In this period, 386 Decisions have been approved, with an average of 70% validity in the region and of which Argentina incorporated 81%. Regarding Resolutions, 1064 have been approved, with a validity index of 66%, having internalized my country 83%; and as regards the Directives, 146 were approved between 1994 and 2004, of which 75% are in force in the Member States, with 80% of them adopting Argentina14.

This shows that gradually the situation regarding the validity of the community rules has improved, an improvement that we hope will intensify.

In spite of this, the concern already expressed about the fact that we are referring to norms adopted by consensus of the representatives of our four countries remains valid.

To overcome this situation, the dictation of Decision n. 22/04 that establishes a mechanism for the purpose of the validity and application in the States Parties of the Decisions, Resolutions and Directives of the Mercosur bodies with decision-making capacity that do not require legislative approval. This procedure includes conducting internal consultations and analysis of legal consistency, and it is of the greatest importance that it be regulated in the countries of the zone. (...)

In the system of the European Union, the Court of Justice of the European Communities holds the supreme and exclusive judicial power for the resolution of all questions relating to Community law. Its general mission is described as follows: "The Court of Justice guarantees respect for the Law in the interpretation and application of this Treaty" (Article 220 of the EEC Treaty).

This general description of its mission covers the following key areas: 1. Control of the application of Community law both by the Community institutions when implementing the provisions of the Treaties, as well as by the Member States and individuals in what is referred to to the fulfillment of its obligations derived from Community law; 2. Interpretation of Community law; 3. Development of community law.

The Court of Justice of the European Communities carries out this mission within the framework of both a consultative and a judicial function.2 This fundamental role played by European justice3 has been possible because it has been understood that the right is embodied in its application by the judicial bodies. Judicial, it is there where it is manifested and demonstrates its effectiveness, we have an equal responsibility. (...)

The Protocol of Ouro Preto - POP meant the adaptation of the institutional structure, and an institutional transformation by granting international legal status to Mercosur. Through art. 53 of the Protocol provided for the repeal "(...) of all the provisions of the Treaty of Asunción, of March 26, 1991, which are contrary to the terms of this

Protocol and to the terms of the Decisions approved by the Common Market Council during the transition period. " It meant therefore a reform of the Treaty of Asunción and an incorporation of provisions that are no longer in the structure of the Protocol but that assume the form of original sources to which the provisions dictated by the organs must be subject. (...)

This incorporation takes place through the competent internal bodies according to the area to which the regulations correspond, except in cases where there is no need for ratification or specific agreement of the Common Market Council. The Protocol of Ouro Preto in its article 40 established a procedure seeking to guarantee the simultaneous validity in the States involved of the rules issued by Mercosur:

I - Once the norm is approved, the States Parties will adopt the necessary measures for its incorporation into the national legal order and will communicate them to the Administrative Secretariat of Mercosur;

II - When all the States Parties have informed the incorporation to their respective internal legal systems, the administrative secretariat of Mercosur will communicate the fact to each State Party;

III - The norms will come into force simultaneously in the States Parties 30 days after the date of communication made by the Administrative Secretariat of Mercosur, in the terms of the previous literal. To that end, the States Parties, within the aforementioned period, will publicize the beginning of the validity of said standards, through their respective official journals. (...)

The excellent work done by Alejandro Perotti and Deisy Ventura - both from the Technical Secretariat of Mercosur - in the book The Legislative Process of Mercosur, 6 they state:

(...) very often it happens that a norm incorporated into the national law of a country, and theoretically in force in it, is not applicable in another because it has not proceeded yet to receive the Mercosur norm for its system legal.

The lack of determination of the cases in which the incorporation process should be followed, that is, the hypothesis in which recourse must be had to the provision analyzed (Article 40), which is saved by Article 42 of the Protocol. Said article clearly recognizes that there are cases in which the derived Mercosur norm will not need its previous incorporation into domestic law to become effective and be fully applicable, both within Mercosur and in the territory of each of the Member States, by the authorities with competence to do so.

The rule, generality - as it arises from the literal wording of Article 42 -, is the unnecessaryness of internalization; At the same time, the requirement of transposition or enforcement in national law constitutes an exception and, therefore, it should be interpreted restrictively. In case of doubt, you should be in doubt about the acceptance of the immediate effect (...)

Mr. Daniel Ibérico Gutierrez Proto, President of the Supreme Court of Justina of Uruguay:

(...) In this context, entering the panorama of application of Mercosur rules in Uruguay, I must specify that a situation similar to that posed by the President of the Supreme Federal Court of Brazil, regarding his country, is registered in our country. In Uruguay, the treaties are signed and signed by the Executive Power and later ratified or not, by the Legislative Power with whose ratification operates the entry of the treaty into the national legal order, with force of law, of equal rank in the regulatory pyramid - by under the Constitution of the Republic - that the ordinary laws and, as such, are applicable by the jurisdictional organs, both those that make up the Judicial Power and those external to it. "

From the speech of the Supreme Court Minister in Argentina, it has been proved that the Treaties have either constitutional hierarchy or are supra legal. This is also what Julio Barboza says (2003: 77):

"The new Constitution has made classifications. All the treaties are "supreme law of the Nation", according to Article 31 of the CN, for belonging to federal law, which has preeminence over provincial rights. But some will have a constitutional hierarchy and others will be purely supralegal.

(...)

The international human rights instruments explicitly mentioned in article 75, section 22, and those that in the future include the Congress with the vote of two thirds of the totality of the members of each Chamber, have a constitutional hierarchy.

In Brazil, paragraph 3 of article 5 (see item 2.1, Table: **The hierarchy of treaties in the Mercosur constitutions**) is totally symmetrical with Article 31 of the Argentine Constitution of 1994, when it states that the Human Rights Treaties have a constitutional hierarchy, implying that the other treaties are supra-legal with the status of ordinary law.

In Paraguay, Article 137 establishes a legal order in which the constitution is the top, followed by higher laws and lower laws in which treaties, conventions and international agreements approved and ratified have the status of higher law.

In Uruguay, Article 6 welcomes international treaties. However, it should be mentioned that the charter does not mention the hierarchy of treaties. Here is the text of the cited article:

"Article 6°.- In the international treaties that the Republic celebrates, it will propose the clause that all differences that arise between the contracting parties will be decided by arbitration or other peaceful means. The Republic will seek the social and economic integration of the Latin American States, especially as regards the common defense of their products and raw materials. Likewise, it will tend to the effective complementation of its public services. "

The combination of Article 6 and 239 transcript leads us to the following conclusion:

1– Treaties are federal laws, in their scope; and
2– The rights and obligations arising therefrom fall within the jurisdiction of the Supreme Court of Justice, so they are courts of final judicial jurisdiction.

In this way, it can be inferred that in Uruguay the treaties have, at least, an infra constitutional hierarchy of higher law.

In Venezuela, article 23 of its Constitution (see item 2.1, Table: The hierarchy of treaties in the Mercosur constitutions) reveals that the Treaties have constitutional hierarchy and that they prevail in the internal order.

From the speeches of the presidents of the supreme Southern Courts, jurists and professors, which we transcribe, we can say that there is a hierarchical symmetry of the international treaties and the establishment of a Permanent Court of criminal and administrative-disciplinary jurisdiction is a politically and juridically viable proposal.

CHAPTER 3

Constitutional References on Corruption in Mercosur

In this chapter, we investigate the existence of objective references onto corruption with public money in the texts of the constitutions of Mercosur member countries.

Let us not confuse the simple literal constitutional reference onto corruption, with corruption of constitutional justice. On this, we have the following reexamination of the forum promoted by "ASSOCIATION OF MAGISTRATES OF URUGUAY, April 1998 Montevideo. The judicial power against corruption "(1998: 74-75):

> "But it does not stay here. In another passage, Cappelletti a rma: that is how constitutional justice, far from being, by its nature, contrary to democracy and the will of the majority, stands as a fundamental instrument to protect the principles of democracy and democracy. of the majority against a risk of corruption. Our democratic ideal does not lead us to admit that the will of the majority is omnipotent; our philosophy does not admit that everything in life can be questioned (15).

> Great company of corruption, risk of corruption, are the textual expressions of the illustrious professor. (...)

> The strongest attacks on the bastion of constitutional justice usually start from conceptions derived from a misunderstood democracy, according to which the

government programs, the programs elaborated by the political powers that, in turn, claim to be the most representative organs of the people, when not the only ones, should not be hampered by the judicial bodies whose popular representativeness is, at best, far away, given the regime to which their appointment is subject.

Add to that, another ingredient that derives from an essential note of the democratic regime, which is the periodicity of the mandates, which would not be observed, at least completely, in the judicial sphere. The judicial mandates usually do not have deadlines or, otherwise, only have them with substantially more extensive scopes than those of the President of the Nation and the legislators (16). "

Corruption is a human fact of destructive consequences, deteriorating the integrity of ethical, moral and juridical relations and, therefore, delegitimizing the democratic state of rule, as we know it today.

Corruption is enemy and antithesis of the essence of the State of rule because if it is founded on the law and it is delegitimized by act or state of corruption. Then the state of rule denies itself by permitting the breach of equality of juridical conditions, which, at least in the law, was thought to be possible to achieve from the French Revolution, as Tocqueville (1957.13: 33) explained:

"If, from the eleventh century, we examine what happens in France from fifty to fifty years, at the end of each of these periods, we will not fail to perceive that a double revolution has taken place in the state of society. The nobleman will have descended in the social scale and the ascended peasant. One descends and the other climbs. Nearly half a century brings them closer, and soon they will touch.

And this does not only happen in France. Wherever we direct our gaze, we will notice the same revolution that continues throughout the entire Christian universe. (...)

The gradual development of equality of conditions is, then, a providential event, and has the following characteristics: it is universal, durable, it escapes human authority and all events, like all men, serve for its development. "

We present below a table of literal reference to the existence of constitutional references to corruption in the Mercosur constitutions. As you can see, only Brazil makes express and literal reference to it:

3.1 - Table with constitutional references on corruption in Mercosur

ARGENTINA	There is no
BRAZIL	There is a mention: "Art. 14. Popular sovereignty shall be exercised by universal suffrage and by direct and secret voting, with equal value for all, and, in accordance with the law, by: (...) § 10 - The elective term may be challenged before the Electoral Justice within a period of fifteen days counted from the diploma, instructed the action with evidence of abuse of economic power, corruption or fraud.
PARAGUAI	There is no
URUGUAI	There is no
VENEZUELA	There is no

CHAPTER 4

Constitutional References on Creation of a Supranational Criminal Court in the Mercosur

The creation of International Courts is an aspiration of international law for the solution of supranational conflicts. This pretension found shelter in the creation of regional blocks.

It is in this context that we introduce the idea of unifying the anti-corruption legislation with the conviction that, if there is political-legal will, the means are available, even because the discussion of the International Law on the domain reservation is surpassed, as Antonio Augusto Cançado Trindade (1997: 47) states:

"The domain reservation and the non-exhaustion of domestic remedies have been two procedural exceptions most frequently raised in international litigation: through the first, the requested State tries to prevent consideration of an international level matter by claiming that it falls essentially - mainly in its reserved area or national competence; through the second, the respondent State objects to the consideration of a matter at the international level, alleging that domestic remedies have not been exhausted and that international action is thus granted only after the State has had an opportunity to remedy the alleged damage within its own internal legal system. The present study will deal primarily with the objection of non-exhaustion of domestic remedies per se, nor the exception of reserved domain as such, but rather the interrelationship between the two."

In this sense, we reinforce the existing symmetry between the stisting crimes in the legislation of each Mercosur member country, whose effects extrapolate or can extrapolate their borders without their authors being punished for lack of union of legislation and the creation of a permanent criminal court in Mercosur.

The merging of legislation with the creation of supranational bodies such as a Permanent Criminal Court with Criminal and Administrative-disciplinary jurisdiction in Mercosur can contribute to reducing corruption, by speeding up and concentrating efforts on persecution criminis and in the jus puniendi of the State-administration.

Today, the right to punish and prosecute depend exclusively on cooperation through international Treaties, which discourages the rapid application of the law. On the subject, here is an excerpt of Baigun and Rivas (2006: 147, 149) that deserves consideration:

"D. Cooperation: assistance and extradition

Cooperation among the States Parties, both in regard to assistance and the search for evidence and information, as well as regarding extradition, are the mechanisms that the Convention has designed to carry out its objectives.

In addition to the foregoing, we must point out that from the Document of Buenos Aires, it has the collaboration in the monitoring and implementation of the treaty with the MESICIC (Follow-up Mechanism for Implementation of the Inter-American Convention against Corruption and its group of experts.

Graphically we can develop them in the following way:

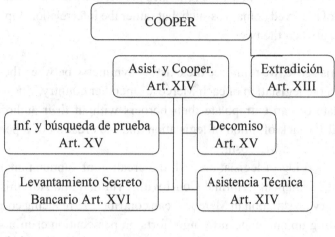

(…)

The formula devised in relation to extradition, aims to prevent requests for extradition are not made under the pretext of invoking the requested official who is a political persecuted, and thus can not be tried in the country of origin, as happened several times (among others, Fujimori). Sign the art. XVII -nature of the act- that:

For the purposes provided in Articles XIII, XIV, XV and XVI of this Convention, the fact that the property obtained or derived from an act of corruption was intended for political purposes or the fact that an act of Corruption has been committed for motivations or for political purposes, alone will not be enough to consider such act as a political crime or as a common crime related to a political crime."

The Supreme Courts of the Mercosur member countries have held meetings to discuss the theme of integration and not that of union as we propose in this work.

The richness of the discussions on integration that address the regionalization of Criminal Law and the creation of a Permanent Criminal Court in Mercosur deserve observation. Here is a summary of what was said in the Supreme Court Forum (2007: 16-20, 22-24):

"Report of the Director of the Mercosur Secretariat to the Common Market Group

2. The role of the Judiciary in consolidating the integration process

The Minister Augusto César Belluscio, Representative of the President of the Supreme Court of Justice of the Argentine Nation, after indicating the articles of the Magna Carta that allow the immediate application of the conventional and customary international norms (articles 31, 116 and 118), described the contribution that the 1994 constitutional reform in Argentina has contributed to integration, especially in terms of the attribution of constitutional status to international norms on the protection of fundamental rights (Article 75, section 22) and the inclusion of a special device, for integration treaties. He also highlighted the constitutional imperative of compliance of treaties with the principles of public law of the Argentine fundamental Charter (Article 27). He pointed out that, in the cases that deal with the application of international standards, it is necessary to verify, first, whether the international standard in question is directly applicable or operative, generating rights and obligations, or whether it is merely programmatic. Next, it is necessary to analyze its compatibility with the principles mentioned in the Constitution; recalling in this sense the Washington Cabrera ruling, on the declaration of unconstitutionality of art. 4 ° of the agreement of Headquarters of the Mixed Technical Commission of Salto Grande, for violation of the fundamental right of access to the jurisdiction. He pointed out that, on several occasions, the Argentine Court applied international source rules, with a prevalence over previous and subsequent laws, indicating some example sentences such as Ekmekdjian c. Sofovich and Fibraca (before the constitutional reform) and Cafés La Virginia (first after the reform).

Dealing specifically with Mercosur law, he drew attention to the fact that the Protocol of Brasilia is not invoked by individuals and explained the operation of the endorsement mechanism of individual litigation by the State. On the other hand, as regards the rules of the block, we considered that the communication of the necessary measures for its application, in the terms of art. 40 Protocol of Ouro Preto, is not required in Argentina, because art. 31 of the Magna Carta allows them to be considered immediately valid in Argentine law, except for the rules of a programmatic nature, in which case the competent bodies have the duty to adopt the necessary norms for its validity. In this way, even when there is no Community right in the Mercosur, in the sense of autonomy and supremacy of the rules of the bloc over those of the internal order, it considers that the mechanism of art. 42 of the Ouro Preto Protocol - from the standpoint of Argentine law - makes the incorporation of operational rules unnecessary, by virtue of the provisions of the aforementioned art. 31 of the Constitution. In any case, it is up to the national judge to apply the Mercosur rules.

Finally, he stressed that the creation of a supranational body, as happened in the European Union, will not lead to the end of the work of the national judges. On the contrary, they will continue to be the ones most responsible for the application of the right to integration, as is the case in the European model. In this way, the preparation of judges for integration - which includes specific training in international law - is fundamental, given their great responsibility to interpret and apply regional regulations, especially due to the lack of precedents and the advent of a new logic that obeys flexible principles such as solidarity, proportionality and subsidiarity.

(...)

In the case of European integration, there was the happy idea of creating a supranational court after the creation of the community itself, forging an engine that accelerated the process. A very peculiar vision of law was established, rendering justice to everyone, from the most humble. The first driving force of the Court of Justice of the European Communities - CJU was the nir rumbos. The legal structure of the U.E. It is a consequence of the action of the court. Armed, thus, that the Executive and the Legislative have every right to say, through the norm, what is best for them, but the judiciary can interpret the commitments and link internal political systems. The Superior Courts of the Member States, in turn, made the necessary efforts to make internal constitutional rights compatible with the requirements of community law.

(...)

In the end, he stressed that it is necessary, for so much, to promote the national juridical structures so that they allow the deep integration on clear bases. Contrary to domestic law, which has a structure of subordination, international law needs to be permanently justified to itself, because it has no dogmatic and because it is subject to changes that require a joint analysis of the system of public international law (DIP), that demands from the judges the domain of the DIP, from the justice of the peace to the Minister of the Supreme Court.

(...)

3. Experience of the Court of Justice of the European Union

National courts, in turn, gradually adapted to community jurisprudence. Being the right of first generation, the integrated Europe was already in the 1980s. It was time to ask How to demonstrate to the State its duty to submit to community decisions? I emphasize that the most sensitive part, in people and in the States, is the pocket, for which the principle of civil responsibility for the breach of community law, enshrined in the Francovich case, was created.

Professor Cecilia Fresnedo, from the University of the Republic. Uruguayan, first argued that the ECJ not only interprets community law, but also "integrates" the possible gaps that the Community's legal system contains. In this process of integration the Court of Justice is not, however, the exclusive interpreter of Community law - since also the judges of the Member States have the capacity to interpret this right - more if it is the "supreme" on this point. Based on the analysis of the preliminary ruling mechanism, according to the ECA, and the possibility of its transpolation to the Mercosur scheme, it affirmed that even under the Protocol of Olivos it is not foreseen that the national judges of the Member States will submit consultations on the interpretation of Mercosur law to the Permanent Review Court; However, as provided by the same Protocol, the system must be developed in this direction.

(...)

To this affirmation, Minister Kemelmajer replied, arguing that the "political courage" to assume what we have to assume is perhaps absent from the process. Through community mechanisms, integration occurs more quickly. He stressed that, if we were more integrated, the Argentine crisis would probably not have taken place with the scope with which it occurred, since the mechanisms of macroeconomic coordination would have avoided the attachment to the exchange rate parity. He noted that, given that the European mechanism works, it is not about copying it, but about taking a step forward, taking into account the legal instruments available. Finally, he urged the actors that have decision-making power in the Mercosur area to abandon the busy stage of the proposals and declarations, acquire the necessary courage to institutionalize a permanent Court of Justice for the bloc, in the style of established in Europe, as a way to accelerate the development of Mercosur."

At the outset, with a view to establishing a Tribunal with permanent jurisdiction in Mercosur, it was said:

"4. Perspectives for the creation of a permanent legal institution in Mercosur

The third panel of the event, according to the program, aimed to "examine the possibility of creating a permanent organ in the structure of Mercosur. Given the intergovernmental nature of Mercosur and the current stage of integration, the rules generated in the bloc will always be subject to the real possibility that they will be considered unconstitutional or in conflict with domestic legal systems." Thus, the debate should address the way "fill the gap of a legal body, which could have the power to anticipate, in advance, even as a consultant, greater security in the hypothesis of emergence of future controversies."

The table was chaired by Minister Adolfo Roberto Vázquez, of the Supreme Court of Justice of the Argentine Nation, who presented the text "Prospects for the creation of a permanent legal institution." The document supports the "need for the establishment of supranational bodies for the Common Market of the South and, in particular, a Supranational Court of Justice, to achieve a harmonious interpretation, unification and application of the rules of community law, so as to consolidate legal security and the effectiveness of dispute settlement mechanisms."

Minister Vázquez pondered that the creation of these bodies would not imply loss of sovereignty, but its accretion, because it would allow us to approach the great geographical and political centers, which are leaving the mark of their configuration in the world. Then, he brought to the debate some general lessons on the theory of economic integration and European community law. He also mentioned the Argentine jurisprudential evolution in international and integration matters.

Finally, recalling the Ouro Preto Charter, prepared by the platinic magistrature on September 21, 1996, he advocated: I) the adaptation of the constitutional norms of the member states to the principle of the primacy of community law; II) the incorporation into the Treaty of Asunción of an express prescription consecrating the rule of supremacy of community law over national rights; III) the direct and immediate amplification of the community norms by the jurisdictional bodies and the national authorities; IV) the creation and installation of a Supranational Court of Justice for the application, interpretation and jurisprudential unification of community law.

(...)

"Among the possible functions of the Supreme Courts Commission, would be to promote assistance and cooperation between national courts: the exchange of information and experiences on the application of Mercosur regulations; the joint consideration with the Ministries of Justice of the creation of instruments that facilitate economic operations; and alert national judges on the di culties of application of the regulations in question.

The proposed entity would guarantee, in this way, the closest approximation of national justice to the integration process, seeking to promote inter-institutional agreements between the different areas of the Judicial Powers and favor the future establishment of a permanent judicial institution in Mercosur. "

It remains evident from the discussions between the Judiciary branches and from the participation of representatives of the Legislative branch in the meetings of Supreme Courts of countries of Mercosur, that there is legislative symmetry, a pretension to regionalise Criminal Law and to create a Permanent Criminal Court.

The big question is: is there political-legal courage to implement a project that will surely will strike down corruption to the tolerable minimum limits and hurt the private interests of those who live by plundering the public treasury?

4.1 - Table 1 – Existing Constitutional references on the creation of a supranational court in Mercosur

We did a comparative study in the constitutions of Mercosur member countries and we did not find explicit references to the creation of a supranational court. Here is the result:

ARGENTINA	There is no express reference.
BRAZIL	There is no express reference.
PARAGUAI	There is no express reference.
URUGUAI	There is no express reference.
VENEZUELA	There is no express reference.

On the other hand, with the exception of the legislation of Brazil and Paraguay, there are explicit and implicit references to the acceptance of a supranational order, as can be seen from the table below:

4.2 - Table 2 — Existing Constitutional references on the acceptance of a supranational legal order in Mercosur

ARGENTINA	THERE IS EXPRESS REFERENCE TO THE ACCEPTANCE OF AN SUPRAESTATAL OR SUPRANATIONAL ORDER: "Article 75. - Corresponds to the Congress: (...) 24. Approve integration treaties that delegate powers and jurisdiction to supra-state organizations in conditions of reciprocity and equality, and that respect the democratic order and human rights. The norms dictated in their consequence have hierarchy superior to the laws. The approval of these treaties with Latin American States will require an absolute majority of the totality of the members of each Chamber. In the case of treaties with other States, the Congress of the Nation, with the absolute majority of the members present in each House, will declare the convenience of the approval of the treaty and can only be approved with the vote of the absolute majority of the whole of the members of each House, after one hundred and twenty days of the declaratory act. The denunciation of the treaties referred to in this clause will require the prior approval of the absolute majority of the totality of the members of each Chamber.
URUGUAI	There is not. The art. 6 of the Uruguayan constitution is not sufficient to guarantee a supranational order. "Article 6.- In the international treaties that the Republic holds, it shall propose the clause that all differences arising between the contracting parties shall be decided by arbitration or other peaceful means. The Republic will seek the social and economic integration of the Latin American States, especially as regards the

	common defense of their products and raw materials. Likewise, it will promote the effective complementation of its public services. "
VENEZUELA	Article 153. The Republic will promote and favor Latin American and Caribbean integration, in order to move towards the creation of a community of nations, defending the economic, social, cultural, political and environmental interests of the region. The Republic may sign international treaties that combine and coordinate efforts to promote the common development of our nations, and that ensure the welfare of the peoples and the collective security of its inhabitants. For these purposes, the Republic may attribute to supranational organizations, through treaties, the exercise of the necessary competencies to carry out these integration processes. Within the policies of integration and union with Latin America and the Caribbean, the Republic will privilege relations with Latin America, trying to be a common policy of all our Latin America. The rules adopted in the framework of the integration agreements will be considered an integral part of the current legal system and of direct and preferential application to domestic legislation.

In short, Argentina and Paraguay make explicit reference, and Brazil, Uruguay, and Venezuela make an implicit constitutional reference to the acceptance of a supra national or supranational order.

The Supreme Courts of Mercosur have a concurring opinion regarding the acceptance of a Supranational Court, as we gather from the annals of their meetings (2007: 23,35,62,74-7781,88):

"4. Perspectives for the creation of a permanent legal institution in Mercosur

The third panel of the event, according to the program, aimed to "examine the possibility of creating a permanent body in the structure of Mercosur. Given the intergovernmental nature of Mercosur and the current stage of integration, the rules generated in the bloc will always be subject to the real possibility that they will be considered unconstitutional or in conflict with domestic legal systems." Thus, the debate should address the way "fill the gap of a legal body, which could have the power to anticipate, in advance, even as a consultant, greater security in the hypothesis of emergence of future controversies."

(...)

Finally, recalling the Ouro Preto Charter, prepared by the platinic magistrature on September 21, 1996, he advocated: i) the adaptation of the constitutional norms of the member states to the principle of the primacy of community law; ii) the incorporation into the Treaty of Asunción of an express prescription consecrating the rule of the supremacy of community law over national rights; iii) direct and immediate amplification of Community rules by the courts and authorities; national iv) the creation and installation of a Supranational Court of Justice for the application, interpretation and jurisprudential unification of community law.

(...)

2nd MEETING OF SUPREME COURTS OF MERCOSUR STATES PARTIES AND ASSOCIATES

(...) In this sense, the Second Meeting of Supreme Courts of Mercosur is held at a very opportune moment, since the treatment of the institutional theme requires the effective participation of the Judiciary Powers, in particular the Supreme Courts of the States Parties in the regional integration process.

(...)

With regard to the recent institutional developments related to the National Judiciary, the importance of the creation of the Permanent Review Tribunal, whose President, Ambassador José Antônio Runelli, is worth mentioning, in the framework of the Olivos Protocol, Which, although it is not effectively to Mercosur judiciary as such, is a permanent forum for the purpose of resolving disputes between the States Parties.

Among many other examples, the accord that has just been signed a few days ago on the fight against piracy in Mercosur deserves a record of its direct relevance to the judicial area. The instrument counted on the adhesion of Bolivia, Chile and Peru, already associated States of the Mercosul, and will represent milestone in the collaboration between these countries to reduce illicit activities.

PROFESSOR LUIZ ROBERTO BARROSO - (...) The question is whether or not the creation of supranational institutions in Brazil depends on the issue of a specific constitutional norm.

Professor and Minister Gilmar Mendes advocates the thesis that it is possible to extract from the sole paragraph of art. However, I did not read any text to that effect. Therefore, this is the authoritative opinion of a Minister of the Federal Supreme Court.

Nevertheless, it is well to see that the sole paragraph of article 1, although it advocates the creation of such a mechanism within Mercosur, it materializes in a programmatic norm that does not explicit mechanisms for the realization of this integration. Therefore, in theory, there is a real risk of Brazilian law, the lack of a constitutional basis for these supranational institutions.

Therefore, Madam President and Rapporteurs, the position of our committee is that a constructive interpretation of the sole paragraph of art. To supranational institutions. Therefore, we do not close the door to what exists, but we believe that this door needs to be carved in a more specific way and that is possible, without margin to answer, to give rise to the establishment of such bodies. (...)

PANEL II - JUDICIAL COOPERATION: THE LORD MINISTER CARLOS BRITTO (SUPREME FEDERAL COURT): So, for example, our Constitution makes Mercosur, incorporating countries that are parties to the pact and associated countries, an obligatory trail, an obligatory governmental path to follow. It is one of the aspects by which our Brazilian Constitution gains the title of Director, because it is prepared to direct the political nucleus of the Power.

In other words, it is a constitution that intends to govern the one who governs, directs the one who directs, in this perspective of the formation of a Latin American community of nations; and then, perhaps, organically, we will organically have the opportunity to experience reinvention as a way of life, enabling us all, Latin American brothers, to constant rebirth within ourselves. The Brazilian instruments that we have, we have as excellent: it is this redemptive Constitution of 1988. (...)

PROFESSOR ANTENOR MADRUGA: The first question is whether the current normative set is sufficient to promote ample judicial cooperation between the States Parties and associates of Mercosur. The second question is whether, in judicial cooperation in Mercosur, it would be desirable for the prior examination of a public order offense and sovereignty to grant exequatur or homologation of a foreign judgment to be carried out diffusely. And the third question, whether before the constitutions of the Mercosur States Parties, is it possible to accept foreign judgments for criminal purposes, such as corruption, impediment of assets or application of restrictive sentences of liberty, the In the light of these three questions, it is first of all for me

64

to demonstrate what the Supreme Court thinks about the question of international legal cooperation.

The reading of the decision of the Federal Supreme Court, in Rogatory Letter 10.484, which was judged a little more than a year ago, on October 23, 2003, demonstrates its position in relation to letters rogatory, which the Court itself classifies as enforceable letters or letters rogatory. In the example of this letter of letters, Switzerland asked for cooperation with Brazil in order to obtain a breach of bank secrecy and seizure of assets in Brazil, which were indispensable measures for an investigation conducted by Switzerland on the trafficking of women in Brazil to Switzerland. The position of the Supreme Court in this case was as follows: "The proceedings for the seizure of assets and breach of data, in addition to violating public order, are enforceable, which makes it impossible to grant exequatur." That is, this is not an isolated decision of the Supreme; it is a repeated application of jurisprudence, in which the Supreme Court has denied international cooperation, in view of the enforceability of decisions.

This has caused some problems for Brazil because the rogatory letter is also a means by which Brazil calls for cooperation with several other States and there is this Supreme jurisprudence. It has been easier to obtain, and it is a paradox, Brazil's international cooperation for the extradition of people than to break their bank secrecy or to kidnap assets. (...)

With regard to the second question: in judicial cooperation within Mercosur, would it be desirable to have a prior examination of an offense against public order or sovereignty, in order to grant an exemption or homologation of a foreign judgment, be carried out in a diffuse manner?

The group understood that Brazil's current position of concentrating this decision-making process - today, in the

Supreme Court and tomorrow in the STJ - is a system that does not find shelter in most countries and which leads to important courts, such as ours Constitutional Court and our Superior Court of Justice, to have to be concerned with cases such as: ratification of divorce judgments or acts of mere record.

The fact is that this remains, in spite of some treaties - including within Mercosur - to allow the direct sending, for example, of rogatory letters in frontier regions, from judge to judge. The Supreme has already considered this unconstitutional, in view of the rule of article 102, "h", which determines the competence of the Federal Supreme Court to approve letters rogatory. So if a judge at the border with Brazil has to send a letter and needs to hear a witness or quote someone on the other side of the border, he must send that letter rogatory to Brasilia; Brasília sends her to Montevideo - in the case of Uruguay; the exequatur is given; and goes to the border, to the judge across the street. This has happened and the idea of turning this judgment of concentrated deliberation into one of diffuse deliberation should not be very strange, because, for example, the Law of Introduction, in its article 17, states:

"Art. 17 - The laws, acts and judgments of another country, as well as any declarations of will, will not be in Brazil when they offend national sovereignty, public order and good customs."

With regard to acts and sentences, this is a concentrated deliberation, but the Brazilian judge, every day, applies foreign law making the same judgment of violation of public order, sovereignty and morality - as the law - without this being diffused, and does it very well. There are, of course, positive points in the concentration and there are good points in making this judgment diffuse, but the consensus in the Group is that the ideal would be to be exercised in a diffuse way.

Lastly, last point for consideration: in view of the constitutions of MERCOSUR States Parties, is it possible to ratify foreign judgments for criminal purposes, such as conspiracy, impediment of assets or application of custodial sentences?

Someone has already said that Public Law enforcement from another state is a real taboo. Brazil allows the homologation of foreign criminal sentences basically for the application of security measures and for their civil effects. Therefore, it does not permit the homologation of foreign criminal sentences, which is not in line with the demand that this globalized world demands, in order to give effect to the jurisdictional power of each State.

Within the European Union, there is already the ratification of foreign criminal sentences, more and more the issue of the impediment of property, the homologation of the criminal effect of preventing property is necessary as the fight against crime as money laundering. Therefore, the question that arises is if it is possible before the Constitutions of the Mercosur Member States. In the case of Brazil, what is interpreted is that there is an infra constitutional disposition, only available to the Criminal Code, but there would be no obstacle, unless a better judgment, that a treaty could allow the ratification of foreign criminal sentences for the purpose of such a treaty, impediment of property or even the application of sentences restricting freedom.

When one sees, for example, the transfer of persons only - this is already quite common - is nothing more than the fulfillment in Brazil of a foreign criminal sentence. (...)

Ms. Nádia de Araújo, from Pontifícia Católica University of Rio de Janeiro: In the cooperation system, very little progress has been made. This legal Mercosur regarding cooperation, in fact, is Mercosur that has advanced, is the Mercosur that, I would say, works. Even when it comes to the death of Mercosur, in the Mercosur dioceses, relaunching the Mercosur, it is forgotten that, since the 90s, they are in force: Protocol of Las Leñas, often used by the Supreme Court, the Protocol of Precautionary Measures and the Buenos Aires Protocol on National Jurisdiction, in addition to all harmonized rules of private international law, derived from the OAS, of the Inter-American Conventions, which are often already internalized in four countries.

José Raul Torres Kirsmser, Vice-President of the Supreme Court of Justice of Paraguay: The Protocol of Las Leñas on Cooperation and Jurisdictional Assistance in Civil, Commercial, Labor and Administrative Matters, among the States Parties of Mercosur, was approved by the Decision of the Common Market Council n. 05/92, ratified by the Argentine Republic on July 3, 1996, by the Federative Republic of Brazil on February 16, 1996, by the Republic of Paraguay on September 12, 1995, and by the Oriental Republic of Uruguay on the 15th. July 1998, is currently in force among all the signatories of the Treaty of Asunción.

As I pointed out that there were international instruments on the subject, we can cite as sources of this Protocol, the Inter-American Conventions of Panama of 1975 on letters rogatory and on receipt of evidence abroad, the Montevideo Convention of 1979, on receipt of evidence in foreign law and on letters rogatory, the Uruguayan, Brazilian and Argentine-Brazilian agreements on judicial cooperation in 1991.

What is this Protocol looking for? An adequate jurisdictional cooperation between the States Parties to the Treaty of Asunción, in order to administer justice in each of them, to contribute to the equitable treatment of its citizens and permanent residents, and to facilitate the free access to jurisdiction in those States for the defense of their rights and interests and achieve legal security.

It is expressed in the preamble that is intended to strengthen the integration process and promote and intensify judicial cooperation in civil, commercial, labor and administrative matters in order to contribute in this way to the development of its integration relations based on the principles and respect for national sovereignty, equality of rights and reciprocal interests and thus achieve the objectives of the Treaty of Asunción.

This Protocol provides for the designation of a central authority that will be appointed by each State Party, which will be responsible for receiving and processing requests for jurisdictional assistance. There are many issues that are dealt with or that are legislated in this Protocol but for reasons of time we will only refer to the impact and practical application of some of its provisions. Regarding the application of the foreign law office in Paraguay, Article 22 of our Civil Code establishes the principle that foreign law has been incorporated into our legal regime. This means that, with their incorporation, the judges have to apply de o cio. With this change in our new legislation, a totally adverse, contrary system has been modified, where only the foreign law could be applied at the request of parties and the burden of proof was left to the parties. At the present time, the judge must apply ex officio. The current standard says:

Article 22. Judges and courts shall apply ex officio the foreign laws, provided that they do not oppose political institutions, laws of public order, morality and good customs, without prejudice to the parties being able to claim and prove the existence and content of them.

This Las Leñas Protocol, in accordance with Article 22 of the Paraguayan Civil Code, facilitates the issue by legislating on information on foreign law. Regarding the procedure to be followed to obtain such information, article 28 provides that:

The central authorities of the States Parties shall be provided as judicial cooperation and provided that they do not oppose the provisions of their public order, reports in civil, commercial, labor, administrative and private international law matters, without any expense...)

To Senhora Minister Elena Highton de Nolasco, gives the Supreme Court of Justina da Argentina: Globalization and integration processes that involve the transnationalization of capital, investment and labor forces as well as a living vehicle for the exchange of cultures, as well they involve the challenge of finding suitable instruments of judicial cooperation that can, that allow facing the internationalization of the crime or the persecution of those responsible for an offense committed in domestic jurisdiction when it has crossed the border.

Hence, it is essential to find mechanisms that allow the judicial powers of the States Parties to have a sense of continuity beyond borders. At the European level, the Schengen Convention pioneered, which initially ruled out the vicissitudes of both judicial and police cooperation, thus serving as an essential input when such competence reaches the community level. The gradual development of Mercosur has produced an increase in legal interaction among its inhabitants, thus increasing the number of processes promoted that require the assistance of the administration of justice. (...)

For its part, in the Mercosur, the Las Leñas Protocol on jurisdictional assistance in civil, commercial, labor and administrative matters and the Convention on precautionary measures, Ouro Preto Protocol, are in force.

4.3 — Norms that have immediate and obligatory application in the scope of Mercosur

There are studies that indicate within the integration process, the existence of rules of immediate application, as shown by Inés Martínez Valinotti, PhD la Universidad Nacional de Asunción, in the cited forum (2007: 27-28):

"Continuing, Dr. Inés Martínez Valinotti, Professor at the National University of Asunción, presented a synthesis of Mercosur's rules of law that discipline the incorporation of Mercosur legal rules into the internal order of the member states. He mentioned, among other things, the provisions of the MAGP (articles 38, 40 and 42) and, in relation to the rules of secondary legislation, various Decisions of the CMC and resolutions of the GMC. He referred to the Draft Protocol on the immediate incorporation of administrative regulations that do not require legislative approval, presented by the Argentine Delegation and in the process of negotiation within Mercosur.

With regard to judicial practice, he highlighted the recent sentence of the justice of Paraguay, which immediately applied the Regulation of the Recife Agreement (on Integrated Border Controls between the Mercosur Countries), signed between Argentina and Paraguay, which has not yet had been internalized by the signatory States. Regarding the "jurisprudence" of the ad hoc arbitration tribunal on the incorporation of norms, it analyzed the scope of Awards IV (Brazil-Argentina, on intra-zone anti-dumping duties) and VII (Argentina-Brazil, on incorporation of GMC Resolutions - tosanitarios), highlighting the distinction made by the Court between the "obligatory nature" and the "validity" of the rules derived from Mercosur law, as well as the obligations "to do" and "not to do" imposed on the member states by the law mercosureño and the concept of "reasonable term" of internalization of nest by the arbitral jurisprudence."

We also recall that our proposal in this work goes to step further by integrating, by proposing the unification of criminal, administrative, and administrative disciplinary legislation, with the creation of a Permanent Court of Criminal and Administrative Jurisdiction, which can be accomplished with the conclusion of a treaty providing that each country promotes symmetry in the few cases in which it does not exist.

Here are some dialogues between the Supreme Courts of the Mercosur countries, in which they were identified and distinguished asymmetries and constitutional symmetries:

"Mr. Alejandro Daniel Perotti, from the Secretary of Mercosul: With regard to the transfer of competencies and direct application, there is much talk of asymmetries as if it were a negative word, asymmetry, the only thing that means is difference, that is, Asymmetry does not mean an obstacle to integration, but a difference in regulation.

If one-steps down, the four Constitutions of the Mercosur countries constitutionally recognize the process of integration, that is, in the four Constitutions we have clauses that refer to the integration treaties. First conclusion: obviously, there are differences between the regulations of Argentina, Paraguay, Uruguay and Brazil, but these differences are here called less precision, that is, the constitutional norms of Uruguay and Brazil are less specific, as to what they mean for the constitution of integration. (...)

"The imperativeness and obligatory nature of the right that is born of the integration treaties would not find their foundation in the attitude of the other States Parties and regional bodies but in the objective of integration. For this reason, the meaning of article 2 of the Treaty of Asunción is to guarantee that the loyal and effective observance of the right of integration constitutes a mandate that each country assumes in relation to the rest of the States, which ultimately generates the duty to faithfully comply with the order of integration, at the head of the obligated country and the right of others to demand such compliance through the channels established for such n, for example: the Treaty of Asunción and its derived right through of the mechanism established in the Olivos Protocol, this is corroborated by Article 38 of the Protocol of Ouro Preto that states in the framework of the Mercosur scheme the principle of loyalty. (...)

I think it is relevant in the point made by the Brazilian Working Group, regarding the constitutional asymmetries of the member countries of Mercosur, coordinated by Minister Gilmar Mendes of the Supreme Federal Court, in which he makes a suggestion:

The harmonization as far as possible of the Brazilian and Uruguayan constitutional texts, with the reforms that occurred in Paraguay in 1992 and in Argentina in 1994, in such a way that it explicitly allows the countries to delegate competence and jurisdiction to supranational bodies with clauses of equality and reciprocity, the hierarchical definition of treaties through rules of primacy that specifically establish the solution of the potential conflict between the treaty and the antecedent or subsequent law, and the establishment of institutional mechanisms of interaction and dialogue between the Executive and Judicial Powers, as soon as there is approval by the Congress of the treaty before the deposit of the instrument of ratification, this to prevent questions of constitutionality control.

However, it should be clarified that this last aspect, this possibility is not viable in the current Argentine constitutional system at least, since the Court is only issued in cases and does not issue general opinions.

The importance of the Brazilian constitutional norm could also be pointed out. The sole paragraph of Article 4, which states that the Federative Republic of Brazil will seek the economic, political, social and cultural integration of the peoples of Latin America, with a view to the formation of a Latin American community of nations. This clear constitutional provision indicates a position more in line with the principles that make up Mercosur and could serve as a reference against the difficulties offered by the internal order regarding the primacy of international agreements. (...)

For its part, Uruguay only has in its memorandum that talking about constitutional impediments is its way of hiding the real obstacle that is the lack of political will. In this way, Uruguay's proposal to use Article 27 of the Vienna Convention on Treaties to find a solution to the constitutional lack of its legal system is a clear indicator of a political will aimed at integration. Hence, Uruguay maintains, in that document, that it is inappropriate to invoke domestic norms as a justification for non-compliance with international obligations, adding that that State ratified the Treaties of Asunción and the Vienna Convention on the Law of Treaties and that, for the principle of irreversibility of the commitments assumed, there is no return. (...)

Professor Jorge Fontoura: In fact, the Brazilian constitutional order does not provide for a prelature norm to regulate confrontation between federal law and an antecedent or later treaty. The reading of the Brazilian constitutional text reveals that, in parallel with the aforementioned absence of norms, treaties can not be understood by an interpretation by eminently analogy as having a hierarchy assimilated to the federal law - letter "a" of item III of article 105 -, therefore, subject to the constitutionality control referred to by Minister Gilmar Mendes - item "b" of item III of art. 102

The Brazilian Supreme Court's jurisprudence on the hierarchy of treaties prevailing in situations of confrontation between law and treaty, antecedent or later, reveals, throughout its history, clear signs that the High Court understands, at least in more recent cases, that in the case of the agreement the later norm prevails.

The lack of regulation of hierarchical discipline between treaty and law on the basis of both the 1988 Constitution and the previous ones brings us the possibility of application by analogy and the understanding that the treaty is equivalent to the law as necessary understanding that it would be possible to assert that the answer before the agreement would be sought, legally, in § 1 of art. (2) of the Law on the Introduction to the Civil Code, which is still in force, and which also concerns the aphorism lex posterior derogatory priori, also cited in the report of the Brazilian group.

It should also be mentioned, among other relevant precedents of the Federal Supreme Court, that in judging Extraordinary Appeal No. 109.173, from the State of São Paulo, the Federal Supreme Court considered that the treaty never prevails over the constitutional text. In the vote of the Minister-Rapporteur, Minister Carlos Madeira, the following reads as follows:

The treaty and law are hierarchically below the Federal Constitution. To accept that a treaty must be respected, including in its possible confrontation as a constitutional text, is to ascribe it, in a political situation, a hierarchy superior to the Political Charter itself, the Constitution.

The Rapporteur concludes by relying on Carlos Maxmiliano: (...) "The constitution is the supreme law of the country, against its letter and spirit, no decisions of federal powers, constitutions, decrees, federal judgments or treaties prevail. or any other diplomatic act. "(...)

Professor Luiz Roberto Barroso: Minister Gilmar Mendes referred to the potentiality offered by the current Brazilian constitutional text in the wording given to the sole paragraph of Article 4, in dealing initially with supranationality, where it reads:

> "Single paragraph. The Federative Republic of Brazil shall seek the economic, political, social and cultural integration of the Latin America, aiming at the formation of a Latin American community of nations."

It is quite possible, with a creative interpretation of this device, to defend Brazil's constitutional legitimacy of the creation of supranational institutions. The truth, however, is that the constitutional provision is far from explicit and, therefore, we will be subject, before the creation of supranational institutions, to questions regarding the norms approved by this institution, because art. 49 of the Brazilian Constitution requires approval by the National Congress and, thus, we would have a constitutional division that would have to be settled with respect to the legitimacy of normative acts produced by supranational instances when interned in the light of this constitutional precept of art. 49.

PANEL II - JUDICIAL COOPERATION

José Raúl Torres Kirmser, Vice-President of the Supreme Court of Justice of Paraguay: I will refer to the topic of constitutional asymmetries. According to the questionnaire they gave us, the following considerations and questions are formulated:

Is it possible to create supranational institutions, or do the constitutional models only allow the attainment of the Asunción treaty limited by the intergovernmental nature of the bloc?

Is it possible that rules produced by Mercosur bodies prevail in confrontation with national legal systems?

In our group we are two, I will refer to the first question, then Dr Roberto will continue with the exhibition.

The problems that may arise due to the constitutional asymmetries of the States Parties in the application of community law due to problems of priority order and in the creation of constitutional bodies for reasons of constitutional asymmetries.

In the first point, our National Constitution does not offer any inconvenience. The rule of article 137 of the Paraguayan Constitution establishes exhaustively: Article 137. The supreme law of the Republic is the Constitution. This, the treaties, conventions and international agreements approved and ratified, the laws passed by Congress and other legal provisions of lower hierarchy, sanctioned accordingly, integrate the positive national law in the order of priority announced.

Whoever tries to change said order, regardless of the procedures provided for in this Constitution, will incur the crimes that will be typified and punished in the law.

This Constitution will not lose its validity nor will it cease to be observed by acts of force or be repealed by any other means than that which it has.

All the provisions or acts of authority opposed to the provisions of this Constitution are invalid.

So this rule is clear in terms of the order of priority listed, of the treaties with respect to national laws, as long as they are ratified and approved by the National Parliament.

Regarding the issue of the creation of supranational bodies we will do a bit of history to observe the positions that were set in the progress of the last years since the signing of the Treaty of Asunción.

The representatives and the Supreme Courts of Justice of Paraguay, Argentina and Uruguay signed the Ouro Preto Charter in September 1996, recommending that the Mercosur States Parties constitute a supranational court of justice to apply, interpret the jurisprudence of community law. It was said at the time that if Brazil decides to adhere to the idea, the government will have to promote constitutional reform through the majority vote of Congress.

The representatives of the highest judicial authorities of these countries recommended a supranational tribunal that decided bindingly on commercial, diplomatic, customs and tax disputes.

In this event, which was the V Meeting of Supreme Courts of the Southern Cone, the representatives of Brazil, including the judicial area and the Executive Branch, expressed that they preferred an arbitration mechanism to resolve disputes in the aforementioned matters and that Mercosur does not need of a court because he lives it as a non-bureaucratic experience. The then Minister of Justice of this brother country indicated in that meeting of judicial magistrates that Brazil's decision on this point will not be reviewed at the moment and that it considered it still very premature to install that supranational body.

Let us remember here that Paraguay was the first country of the Mercosur that in its Constitution of 1992 consecrated a supranational legal order. In its article 145 it expresses this norm:

Article 145. The Republic of Paraguay, under conditions of equality with other States, admits a supranational legal order that guarantees the validity of human rights, peace, justice, cooperation and development, politically and economically, social and cultural.

Said decisions may only be adopted by an absolute majority in each House of Congress.

The same route was followed by the Argentine Republic with the constitutional reform of 1994, including among the attributions of the Congress:

Approve integration treaties that delegate powers and jurisdiction to supranational organizations under conditions of reciprocity and equality, and that respect democratic order and human rights. The norms dictated in their consequence have hierarchy superior to the laws.

Addressing the issue of asymmetries in constitutional matters, let us note that the Magna Carta of Brazil prescribes in its first article:

Article 1° The Federative Republic of Brazil, formed by the indissoluble union of the States, Municipalities and the Federal District, is constituted in a democratic state of law and has the following foundations:

The sovereignty;

The citizenship;

The dignity of the human person;

Social values and work and free initiative;

Political pluralism.

Article 4 of the Constitution of this country in vigorous and promising growth states:

Article 4° The Federative Republic of Brazil is governed in its international relations by the following principles:

National independence,

Prevalence of human rights;

Self-determination of peoples;

Non-intervention;

Equality between the states;

Defense of peace;

Peaceful resolution of conflicts;

Repudiation of terrorism and racism;

Cooperation among peoples for the progress of humanity

- Granting of political asylum.

Sole Paragraph - The Federative Republic of Brazil will seek economic, political, social and cultural integration among the peoples of Latin America, with a view to the formation of a Latin American community of nations.

The Constitution of Uruguay on this subject enshrines in its sixth article:

Article 6 In the international treaties that the Republic celebrates, it will propose the clause that all differences that arise between the contracting parties will be decided by arbitration or other peaceful means. The Republic will seek the social and economic integration of the Latin

American States, especially as regards the common defense of their products and raw materials. Likewise, it will tend to the effective implementation of its public services.

This article necessarily leads us to this question: does the supraley or not accept the principle of supranationality? It is a very dilatory point in this country. Several respected constitutionalists think so, while other experts understand that precisely the text of the constitution must be reformed so that the country can accept decisions of supranational organizations.

The illustrious jurist Dr. Hector Gros Espiell explains: especially the questions concerning the integration of the Latin American states put a necessary international relationship and, therefore, it is admissible that, in relation to it, certain cases the decisions of the international bodies created under treaties or conventions that have been regularly ratified, they have an erga omnes effect directly.

The ex-chancellor Uruguay or warns that, to be possible the existence of international bodies not integrated by Uruguayan representatives and whose decisions are mandatory on Uruguayan land, will require a constitutional adjustment. The eminent jurist adds: "Article 6, paragraph 2, of the Constitution of the Republic authorizes the existence of a community law, allowing the internal public bodies of the State, that is, the Executive Power, which has the competence to sign treaties, and the Legislative Power, which has the power to ratify the treaties, may commit Uruguay as a member of a supranational body, in this case, of the Common Market of the South - MERCOSUR.

We recall that the Ouro Preto Charter reached these conclusions:

I°) The process of integration of the Common Market of the South, as in the other regions, has begun with economic factors and has been oriented towards the exchange of goods and services, and the achievement of a customs union.

2) That, without prejudice to this and as a way of consolidating and regulating the movements of the social and economic cultural area, it is appropriate to address cultural integration, and in this field, the development of community law is essential.

3°) To the recommendations emanated from Meetings of Supreme Courts of Justice of the Southern Cone and without prejudice to the use of peaceful means of self-composition in the resolution of disputes. (...)

"(11-30-2004) PANEL III - HARMONIZED LEGISLATIVE IN MATERIAL AND PROCEDURAL LAW

Mr. Professor Roberto Ruíz Días Labrano (Paraguai): This Mercosur integration process, which was born from the Treaty of Asunción, is strengthened with the Ouro Preto Protocol later and institutionally, part of the idea of building a Common Market. In addition, a common market is inconceivable and the development of an integration process cannot be conceived without the idea of legislative harmonization, not only underlying but linked to the whole task of the development of the integration process. (...)

The construction of a market as such, involve certain necessary aspects that must necessarily be harmonized. There are certain aspects that, in the construction of the market, if they are not there, there is no market. We use the expression "market" in various aspects.

We use it in the sense of place where there is exchange of goods, we use the expression market in the sense that the Treaty of Asunción uses in the construction of an

82

integrated space in which liberties rule, the four classic freedoms: free movement of people, goods, services and capital, plus two essential factors that are the coordination of macroeconomic policies and legislative harmonization.

In this market construction we have to have an idea of what we are building to know what has been done and what is being done in Mercosur. It is intended to build a market, but in what sense. The aim is to build a market on economic bases, starting from economic bases, advancing towards political bases, and sustaining social bases. Therefore, the market idea implies certain necessary disciplines that if the States Parties do not harmonize, do not unite, and then this idea of the market dissolves. There are specific issues of harmonization beyond the harmonization of customs legislation, the harmonization of tariffs, beyond these aspects that are part, in fact, of some basic disciplines in the construction of the market.

There is no market if there is no control of business competition. If there are no clear rules, harmonized rules on how companies and industries are going to participate in the created market, it is difficult to think of a specific market. The first task, therefore, is to harmonize those rules, norms that tend to have clear rules internally in the States, and through a slightly greater task, that is already the unification of the common criteria in this aspect of the construction of the market. In addition, why is the harmonization of competition rules essential? Because competition in the market will imply the economic development of Mercosur or any integration process that pretends to be successful. Great part of the great task of the European Union has been to regulate competition or competition policy as they call it in Brazil. If you follow the rulings of the Court of Justice of the European Communities, you will find that a large part of jurisprudence is based on the application of competition rules in the conflicts generated by the rules of jurisdiction.

Rules that tend to determine, in the first place, what is the limit of action that companies will have, that is, not to admit monopoly rules, not to admit rules of market distortion, not to admit rules in which a company or an industry excludes to another of free competition. The essential foundation of the market is based on free competition. We cannot talk about the single market in Europe; we cannot talk about the common market in Mercosur, if there is no free competition. That is why it is essential not only that all States Parties have adequate domestic legislation on competition, right?, but that it exists as in the case of Paraguay, which is regulated in Article 107 of the national Constitution, Rules are planned. A special rule, a constitutional rule that determines that private monopolies or public monopolies will not be admitted. However, even today we do not have specific legislation on competition.

In Uruguay, the competition rules are still relative, more in-depth legislation is needed, even though the rules that exist today are sufficiently developed in the Uruguayan context to consider that there are competency rules. In Brazil and Argentina, if there is more experience, this means that in essential areas such as these, it is necessary to look for the development of the integration process. (...)

In relation to consumer law we say that it is the counter face of the defense of competition because we are talking about the common citizen, the citizen who is inside an integrated space which we call the common market, or the idea of a common market. We recall that the Mercosul integration process is moving towards a common market, or intends to move towards a common market, but the stage in which we are, we are within an integrated process where there is a market within which the citizen is an essential part of its development. (...)

Other very important areas of harmonization will be the criteria with which the States Parties, through their respective internal legislations and through Mercosur's common legislation, will have to translate in the future to find a compatible integrated space such as the position common against foreign investments. Foreign investments that obviously need guarantees and where there is a counterpoint of interests. The counterpoint of interests is clear for the developed countries, the counterpoint is dissected to the fact that the foreign investment that is eradicated can be eradicated, that is, return to the place of origin, at the moment in which the investor wishes it. (...)

Doctor Ronald Herbert (Uruguai): It is true that it is necessary to harmonize standards in an integration process, but we must be aware of what this integration process consists of and we must be aware that the integration process is dynamic and that it has several stadiums. And that the harmonization of these norms or the quantum of harmonization of these norms depends on the stage in which the process of harmonization is found. So, if we talk about market integration, we are talking about increasing the geographic space of the market. And here, of course, we would have to harmonize the rules regarding the treatment of the relevant factors in the configuration of that market, to which Professor Ruiz Días referred.

It is a matter, this one, in which really much progress has been made in the last decades, therefore, they exist, they have developed, universal criteria and, practically, a universal language. For example, everything that has to do with the customs, tax, health, immigration, central bank, or market protection, as just recently reviewed by Roberto Ruiz Díaz, who have to do with the competition, with the functions of companies, monopolies, abuse of the dominant position, and intuitive laws that are very important such as consumer protection, administration of natural resources, and environmental regulations. (...)

Ms. Elena Highton from Nolasco of the Supreme Court of Justina of Argentina: This issue was addressed by the European Community or the European Union in order to approximate legal systems, through supranational bodies. European Community law is conducted by the administrative, legislative and judicial authorities of each member State, by virtue of the principles of direct applicability and supremacy with a Court that ensures its effectiveness and that functions as an organ that uses interpretation fairly as means of harmonization and unification of the law.

On the other hand, within Mercosur, an intergovernmental system was chosen without imperative power or autonomy. This is chosen as an obstacle in the aspect related to the method adopted for the legislative harmonization in the pertinent areas, this, without ignoring, the mixed nature of the European Union, although it has its supranational aspect in jurisdictional matters. Original formulas should be found so that States can comply with the demanding commitments assumed in the Treaty. It is a project that subordinates certain national interests to the achievement of regional objectives and, therefore, even without transferring powers have, at least in this initial stage, the legifiable possibility, normally recognized to the sovereign States and that here it would be necessary deepen it in the stage, that is, in the aims of integration. In this context difficulties arise, above all, if we bear in mind that the harmonization of law is a truly priority action to be developed for the protection of the economic interests of those who may be harmed by the internationalization of markets. The regulation of responsibilities by the supranational entities tends to eliminate, by means of the coordination of the legislations with the Member States, the inconveniences that the normative disparity existing in each matter consists in the operation of the market itself. The need for an approximation of the laws of the States is justice, as the divergences may distort competition, affect the free movement of goods within the common market and favor the existence of different degrees of protection for those who must acquire and trade within such market. (...)

Professor Eduardo Gleber of the Pontifical Catholic University of Minas Gerais: It is undeniable that a process of economic integration, Mr. President, suffers from the legal instruments intended to give security to legal relations at the international level. The greater or lesser extent of these instruments may limit success or determine the failure of integration to insure as it fails to ensure the protection of the legitimate interests of the parties, whether through the omission of the normative framework of substantive law or through the necessary jurisdictional provision to vindicate them.

On the face of it, there is a need for a reasonable degree of homogeneity regarding the rules of law concerning, for example: contracting, including aspects of delivery, payment of the delay, quality guarantees; as well as, as regards consumer law, the rules of competition, or competence, as the Spaniards say, intellectual property, including protection of copyright and even criminal prosecution, piracy and counterfeiting, among others, whose asymmetry is capable of creating obstacles and distortions detrimental to the functioning of free trade among the economic agents of the States Parties.

Professor Stefania Viveiros (OAB-DF): I do not see, initially, that such Asymmetries of National Judicial Organizations are obstacles to harmonize and standardize the legislative part. As an example, we can cite the very displacement of competence of the Supreme Court to the Superior Court of Justice regarding the homologation of foreign judgments and the granting of exequatur to letters rogatory. This amendment, which was already approved by Congress in the reform of the Judiciary, will leave article 102, letter "h", for article 105, item "i", of the Superior Court of Justice. This displacement did not include who would be competent to carry out such homologation and the granting of exequatur, as stated in item "h" of the Federal Supreme Court. In this way, it will be the responsibility of the STJ's Internal Regulation to appoint or distribute the appropriate competence for such acts. (...)

The second point I make is related to the Firewood Protocol, which was signed in 1992. It is recorded that compliance with the letter rogatory of mere expediency - when I speak of mere expediency, read the hypothesis of citation - will be the responsibility of the foreign exchange authorities. So, in this respect, at least in a theoretical sense, I can foresee, in order to be more effective in this jurisdictional provision, the possibility, theoretically that such jurisdiction should be granted to the first-degree judges, that we are in Front of neighboring countries, which would be much more effective. Therefore, it would be an analysis, seeking the question of effectiveness in the jurisdictional rendering, even because I think that there would be no kind of discretion for the analysis of national sovereignty and the public order carried out by the first-degree judge, as it also happens in applications of foreign laws by the Brazilian judge himself. In this regard, I would have said that I would have an effectiveness with regard to this jurisdictional provision at the time that this first-degree judge could have accomplished the accomplishment of that appointment, as already stated in the Las Leñas Protocol. With this would be integration and a speed in this fulfillment of letters rogatory through these quotations.

Professor Ricardo Alonso García (Spain): Thank you very much, Mr. President. Regarding what my dear friend Berta said, I am not going to enter into a discussion that is really very technical, conceptual of how it is harmonized or how it is left to harmonize and that each one understands by harmonization. In Europe, these are concepts that are clear. One thing is standardization, which means that there is only one standard, which displaces all national law; another thing is harmonization, which implies that the diversity of national legislations is admitted, within common guidelines. In addition, these common guidelines, evidently, mark them as the European norm. What in Europe is very clear that when we talk about harmonization means that we are eliminating national disparities while maintaining a certain diversity within common guidelines. In addition, these common guidelines are included in a European standard. In that clarification, maybe I would like to highlight two essential points, which I think have been coming out throughout all the presentations, but perhaps to facilitate the final report. (...)

That on the one hand, therefore I think it is time to start giving a little, little by little, and for this there is no need to reform any treaty or anything, this is nothing more than having political will rizando certain role to the secretariat, in order to support, I insist, it is not about removing political power, it is about improving the decision-making capacity of who holds the final decision-making power. And in the second place we are going to highlight here, too, it seems to me that it is key, it came out yesterday with the theme of constitutional asymmetries that this is a very important subject.

Who harmonizes? Well, in today who is harmonizing are the executives. That is not to be deceived. Those who harmonize are the executives. And of course, by harmonizing the executives it is evident that one is, because it is neither more nor less, it is repeating here the history that was lived in Europe fifty years ago. This in short, implies that, before harmonization, who is legislating in the States Parties are the parliaments. When you start to harmonize, those parliaments are out of the question because the one who harmonizes are the executives. And what happens, because parliaments have not been associated with this phase of harmonization, when the time comes to internalize, when the time comes to make this harmonization effective, we find ourselves with the sad reality that is what prevails here in Mercosur. And it is simply that the parliaments claim, from my point of view, legitimately claim a role, which have been dispossessed in the negotiation phase (...)

Ms. Professor Claudia Lima Marques - I would like to highlight the important mention of Minister Eros Grau on markets, that is, there is also the need for value our differences. The Brazilian market, of course, has its idiosyncrasies, but it is different from the Uruguayan market - just as an example - and in this sense, the laws that regulate this market, the mentioned economic law of competition and consumer protection. So perhaps thinking more for the future, I think we should see ourselves as international standers, as Minister Elena Highton of Nolasco mentioned. To evolve, we can not lower the level of protection or think that today's reality will be the same as ten years from now. If we want to build a customs union, to Mercosur, we really have to respect the cultural and market differences of each of these countries.

Professor Jaime César Lipovetzky (Argentina): development of a general regulation on labor matters. The labor law of our countries has common standards, but they are different enough to make it necessary to approach a study in such a way that they are unified at a higher level, which is what it is about, and perhaps this implies not only the sanction of norms without or also in the convocation of paritarias, that is to say, for the writing of collective agreements at the level of the four countries and of those that are incorporated in the future, including those that are within the framework of the expanded Mercosur so that, in some way, to begin to work seriously with a view to organizing a common economy within the Mercosur including the macro point of view, and not only micro, a common economy that begins

to solve the problems of dependency and taxation that are
the scourge of most Latin American countries."

We consider it important to emphasize that a full union and integration
in the scope of the countries members of Mercosur requires uniformity and
harmonization of legislation for areas such as:

- Labor law;
- Consumer law;
- Economic law;
- Tax law and others.

I think, as the bloc is a fact, the harmonization of the legislation
represents a step forward in the current conjuncture of acts and state of
corruption that prevails in Mercosur.

So, the the unification of Mercosur's legislation shall cover:

- Criminal legislation;
- Criminal procedural law; and
- Administrative-disciplinary legislation.

Of course, it will be necessary a creation of a Permanent Court of
Criminal and Administrative-disciplinary with jurisdiction, which can be
done from the proven existence of constitutional and infra-constitucional
symmetry and by the hierarchy of international treaties within the
framework of Mercosur, as we have shown.

All of these proposals are factible if the political classes that rule over
Mercosur have political will. As well said Professor Ricardo Alonso García
of Spain:

"This is nothing more than having political will."

CHAPTER 5

Some Brazilian Penal and Administrative Paradigms

The Brazilian Criminal Code devoted its entire Title XI to typify crimes committed by public officials and private individuals against the Public Administration, such as embezzlement, Insertion of false data in the information system Deviation or irregular use of funds or public revenues, extorsion practiced by public officials, passive and active corruption, smuggling or misappropriation of public funds, prevarication, and others, all with full symmetry with the other Mercosur Criminal Codes.

On the other hand, in the sphere of Disciplinary Administrative Law, the Brazilian National Congress decreed and the President sanctioned the Law n° 8.112 / 1990, which devotes the entire TITLE IV to the duties, prohibitions and liabilities of public officials, while TITLE V deals with the Administrative Disciplinary process in any cases of deviation of public officials Ethical conduct.

In more severe cases of Ethical deviation of conduct, like acts of improbity, the Brazilian public officials will be prosecuted according to the commandments of the Law No. 8,429 / 1992, on which we will make comments below.

5.1 - Specific law on the act of improbity in Mercosur

No matter the dictionary you ask for, probity is "the quality of having strong moral principles; honesty and decency."

The significance of the term "probity" invokes honest conduct. Therefore, a law combating improbity in any Public Administration must have as aims to identify and sanction the dishonesty of the conduct of the public official and those who acts in with him in violation of the duties of honesty in dealing with the colective good.

In our comparative study within Mercosur, we find that only Brazil has a law strictly called "Law of acts of improbity".

This does not mean that the other countries do not have laws to combat acts of general misconduct; they just do not have it with such a denomination or with the list of acts as specified by the Brazilian law, which, in such case, can serve as a paradigm for Mercosur and for the world. For the law is good!

Here are examples drawn from Law No. 8,429 / 1992, accessible at www.presidencia.gov.br:

"Of the Acts of Administrative Improbity Impinging Illicit Enrichment

Art. 9 - It is an act of administrative impropriety that implies illicit enrichment to receive any type of improper patrimonial advantage due to the exercise of position, mandate, function, employment or activity in the entities mentioned in article 1 of this law, and in particular:

I - receive, for himself or for others, money, movable or immovable property, or any other direct or indirect economic advantage, by way of commission, percentage, gratuity or gift of direct or indirect interest, which can be reached or protected by action or omission arising from the duties of the public agent;

II - to realize a direct or indirect economic advantage to facilitate the acquisition, exchange or lease of movable or immovable property, or the contracting of services by the entities referred to in art. 1 ° for a price higher than the market value;

III - perceive economic advantage, direct or indirect, to facilitate the alienation, exchange or lease of public good or the provision of service by state entity at a price lower than the market value;

IV - use, in a private work or service, vehicles, machinery, equipment or material of any nature, owned or available to any of the entities mentioned in art. 1 of this law, as well as the work of public servants, employees or third parties contracted by these entities;

V - to receive an economic advantage of any kind, direct or indirect, to tolerate the exploitation or practice of gambling, pimping, narcotics, smuggling, usury or any other illegal activity, or accepting such an advantage;

VI - receive economic advantage of any nature, direct or indirect, to make a false declaration about measurement or evaluation in public works or any other service, or on the quantity, weight, measure, quality or characteristic of goods or goods supplied to any of the entities mentioned in art. 1 of this law;

VII - acquire, for themselves or for others, in the exercise of a mandate, position, job or public function, property of any nature whose value is disproportionate to the evolution of the patrimony or the income of the public agent;

VIII - accepting employment, commissioning or carrying out consultative or advisory activities for an individual or legal entity that has an interest capable of being reached or protected by an action or omission arising from the duties of the public agent, during the activity;

IX - perceive economic advantage to intermediate the liberation or application of public funds of any nature;

X - Receive an economic advantage of any nature, directly or indirectly, to omit an act of office, action or declaration to which he is bound;

XI - incorporate, in any form, assets, rents, funds or amounts that are part of the assets of the entities mentioned in article 1 of this law;

XII - use, for their own benefit, assets, rents, funds or values that are part of the assets of the entities mentioned in article 1 of this law.

Section II

Of the Acts of Administrative Improbity that cause Damage to the Treasury

Art. 10. It is an act of administrative impropriety that causes damage to the treasury any action or omission, willful or guilty, that causes loss of property, diversion, appropriation, maladjustment or dilapidation of the assets or assets of the entities referred to in art. 1 of this law, and in particular:

I - To facilitate or compete in any way for the incorporation of assets, rents, sums or values that are part of the assets and liabilities of the entities mentioned in art. 1 of this law;

II - To permit or compete for the private or legal person to use assets, rents, funds or amounts that are part of the assets of the entities mentioned in art. 1 of this law, without observing the legal or regulatory formalities applicable to the species;

III - To donate to the individual or legal entity as well as to the un-personalized entity, even if educational or assistance, property, income, funds or assets of any of the entities mentioned in art. 1 of this law, without observing the legal and regulatory formalities applicable to the species;

IV - To permit or facilitate the alienation, exchange or lease of assets belonging to any of the entities referred to in art. 1 of this law, or the provision of service by them, at a price lower than the market price;

V - To allow or facilitate the acquisition, exchange or lease of goods or services at a price higher than the market price;

VI - To carry out financial operations without observing the legal and regulatory norms or to accept insufficient or infident guarantee;

VII - To grant administrative or fiscal benefits without observing the legal or regulatory formalities applicable to the species;

VIII - To frustrate the lawfulness of a bidding process or unduly waive it;

IX - To order or permit the execution of expenses not authorized by law or regulation;

X - To act negligently in the collection of tribute or income, as well as with respect to the conservation of the public patrimony;

XI - To release of public funds without strict observance of the relevant rules or in any way for their irregular application;

XII - To permit, facilitate or compete for a third party to become illicitly wounded;

XIII - To allow vehicles, machines, equipment or material of any nature, property or at the disposal of any of the entities mentioned in art. 1 of this law, as well as the work of public servants, employees or third parties contracted by these entities.

XIV -To enter into a contract or other instrument whose purpose is the provision of public services through associated management without observing the formalities provided for by law; (Included by Law No. 11,107 of 2005)

XV -To enter into an agreement for the apportionment of a public consortium without prior consent and without observing the formalities prescribed by law. (Included by Law No. 11,107 of 2005)

Section III

Of the Acts of Administrative Improbability Concerning the Principles of Public Administration

Art. 11. It is an act of administrative impropriety that violates the principles of public administration any action or omission that violates the duties of honesty, impartiality, legality, and loyalty to institutions, and notably:

I - To practice an act forbidden by law or regulation or other than that provided in the rule of jurisdiction;

II - Delaying or failing to act improperly;

III - To reveal the fact or circumstance that he is aware of the attributions and that he must remain in secrecy;

IV - To deny publicity to official acts;

V - To frustrate the lawfulness of public competition;

VI - To cease to be held accountable when required to do so;

VII - By disclosing or permitting the knowledge of a third party, before its respective disclosure, the content of a political or economic measure capable of affecting the price of merchandise, goods or service to be disclosed."

Considering the need to adapt the examples cited to a Mercosur reality, we question: What is the reason for the unification of criminal, procedural penal and administrative-disciplinary legislation, as a means of reducing corruption derived from crimes and acts of administrative improbity that cross the borders of a Mercosur country?

Based on all the factual and political-legal foundations that we have been launching, we believe without any doubt that the union of legislation as we have proposed is capable of reducing corruption with public money, within tolerable limits.

Jorge Luis Rimondi (2005: 273) said about illegal patrimonial increase of public officials in Argentina, the same we can say for the whole of Mercosur and the rest of the world:

"Unfortunately, the existence of public officials that ostensibly increase their personal assets during the exercise of the position seems to be a constant in Argentine history.

At least, this follows from the mere compulsa of the annals of local legislation, in which, throughout the different epochs, the regulations related to the subject are repeated. Thus, for example, on December 5, 1622, King Philip TV dictated Law VII, which established: "(...) governors, corregidores, and alcaldes mayores are not admitted to the use and exercise of their offices, if they shall not present the inventory of all their goods, and having them possessed, and those who are in the Indies shall do so and present themselves before the real audiences of the district (...), "231 supplementing with Act LXVIII insofar as he urged admit in the hearings of the continent to any minister, even before the presentation of the appointment signed by the king himself, if he was not accompanied by the testimony of having presented in the Council of the Indies the inventory of his assets, and the law IX - of the Compilation of the Indies - which provided for the constitution of finances to answer for the subsequent residency trials."

Luis Roberto Gomes (2003: 101) also spoke with propriety that:

"It is worth remembering that, in addition to the constitutional text, infra-constitutional legislation, more precisely Law no. 8,429 / 92, describing in its art. 11 acts of administrative impropriety that violate the principles of public administration, refers not only to "action" but also to "omission" that violates the duties of honesty, impartiality, legality, and loyalty to institutions.

This is indicative of the fact that the administrative omission violating these principles is as harmful as the action, so much, so that it receives the same sanction. That is to say, both the impotent action and the untimely omission result in a legal consequence corresponding to the full compensation of the damage, to the loss of the public function, to the suspension of the political rights, to the payment of a civil fine and to the prohibition of contracting with the Public Power or to receive benefits or credit or credit (Law No. 8.429 / 92, article 12, item III)."

It is convenient to remember for its ethical and moral importance the Brazilian Fiscal Responsibility Law decreed and sanctioned in 2001 and on which Ari Vainer (2001: 7) says:

"The Fiscal Responsibility Law brings about an institutional and cultural change in dealing with public money, society's money. We are generating a rupture in the political-administrative history of the country. We are introducing the budget constraint in Brazilian legislation.

Society no longer tolerates living with irresponsible administrators, and today it is increasingly aware that the citizen, the contributor, pays the bill for the misuse of public money.

The irresponsibility practiced today, at any level of government, will result tomorrow in more taxes, less investments or more inaction, which is the most perverse of taxes because it affects the poorest.
The government does not make money. This statement may seem

obvious to some, but not to those who administer public accounts by spending more than they collect. Leaving debts to their successors and making commitments they know, in advance, they cannot honor. In addition, this type of posture, harmful to the country, which does the Fiscal Responsibility Law curb. The decision to increase expenditure, regardless of merit, must be accompanied by a source of funding."

5.2 - Financial Action Task Force against of Money Laundry (FATF)

The Financial Action Task Force on Money (FATF), also known in the Latin world as GAFI, was founded by the G-7 in 1989. It is an intergovernmental body whose purpose is the development and promotion of policies, both at national and international levels, to combat money laundering and terrorist financing.

This promotion of the development of national and international anti-money laundering programs recognizes the imbricated relation between money laundering and corruption in the Public Sector, offering, among its 49 recommendations, a specific anti-corruption recommendation affiming categorically: "The FATF recognizes the link between corruption and money laundering".

Well, it would be a naive gesture to deny a link between corruption and money laundering.

The IACAC, the UNCAC and the FATF recommendations produced in Brazil the enactment of Law 9,613 / 98, which provides for crimes of "laundering" or concealment of goods, rights and values; the prevention of the use of the financial system for the crimes established in this Law; creates the Financial Activities Control Council – FACC (COAF in Portuguese).

In Argentina, the online edition of 03.06.2011 of the newspaper Clarín reported:

"When the Executive promulgates the sanctioned law yesterday, Argentina will be able to show the world a criminal prosecution other than money laundering. Since 2000, Law 25,246 was in effect, which combated this crime only if another precedent was proven. More clearly:

if a narcotraficante used a figurehead to buy a mansion with money from the drug, it was necessary to advance on contraband to prove the maneuver of money laundering, which was interpreted as a cover-up. Now it will not be necessary because the laundering enters the Penal Code as an autonomous offense."

Well, in June 2011, the Senate and House of Representatives of Argentina approved Law 26,683, which amended the Penal Code, on money laundering. Here is an excerpt of the law:

"ARTICLE 1 - Replace the denomination of chapter XIII, title XI of the Penal Code, which shall be renamed as follows:" Chapter XIII. Concealment".

ARTICLE 2 - Repealed Article 278 of the Criminal Code

ARTICLE 3 - Replace Article 279 of the Criminal Code with the following text:

Article 279: ...

1) If the criminal scale established for the preceding offense is less than that established in the provisions of this chapter, the criminal scale of the preceding offense will be applicable to the case.

2) If the preceding crime was not threatened with a penalty of deprivation of liberty, a fine of one thousand (1,000) pesos to twenty thousand (20,000) pesos or the criminal scale of the preceding crime shall apply, if this was lesser.

3) When the author of the facts described in subsections 1 or 3 of article 277 was a public official who committed the act in the exercise or occasion of his / her duties, he / she will also suffer a special disqualification penalty of three (3) to ten (10) years. The same penalty will be suffered by

anyone who has acted in the exercise of a profession or trade that requires special authorization.

4) The provisions of this chapter shall govern even when the preceding offense was committed outside the spatial scope of this Code, as long as the fact that it was expensive also had been sanctioned with penalty in the place of its commission.

ARTICLE 4 - Incorporate title XIII to the Criminal Code, which will be renamed "Crimes against the economic and financial order".

ARTICLE 5 - Renumber articles 303, 304 and 305 of the Penal Code, as articles 306, 307 and 308 respectively and incorporate the following articles into Title XIII of the Penal Code:

Article 303: ...

1) Shall be punished with imprisonment of three (3) to ten (10) years and a fine of two

(2) Ten (10) times the amount of the transaction, which converts, transfers, manages, sells, taxes, disguises or otherwise puts into circulation in the market, goods derived from a criminal offense, with the possible consequence that the origin of the original goods or surrogates acquire the appearance of a lawful origin, and provided that their value exceeds the sum of three hundred thousand pesos ($ 300,000), either in a single act or by the reiteration of different facts linked together.

2) The penalty provided in paragraph 1 will be increased by one third of the maximum and half of the minimum, in the following cases:

a) When the author performs the act habitually or as a member of an association or band formed for the continued commission of events of this nature;

b) When the author was a public official who had committed the act in the exercise or occasion of his duties. In this case, you will also suffer a penalty of special disqualification from three (3) to ten (10) years. The same penalty will be suffered by anyone who has acted in the exercise of a profession or trade requiring special authorization."

Our bibliographical research has shown a lack of work on corruption and we have not found studies that have proposed the unification of Criminal, Procedural Penal and Administrative-Disciplinary Legislation, dealing with Crimes and Acts of Administrative Improbity against the Public Administration of Mercosur member countries.

In addition, we have not found any other proposal for the legislatures of the world to inscribe in laws acts of corruption with public funds, as crimes against humanity, as we do here. That's a dream! I know it! However, some dreams become reality, no matter the time they will come to came through.

We firmly believe that the unification of legislation as we have proposed can become effective guns to combat corruption with public money and providing a substantive democracy very close to what we are dreaming of, not only for our continent, but also to many parts of the world.

To make this dream a reality, we just need political-juridical will.

CHAPTER 6

Proposal of the Unification of the Legislation to Combat Corruption

The research we carry out shows the existence of national legislation to combat crimes and acts of administrative improbity only within the internal sphere of each member of Mercosur.

As an example, we cite from the legislation of each member country only one article of the Penal Code as indicative of legislation to combat crimes against the Public Administrations:

"Argentine Penal Code

"ARTICLE 261. - The public official shall be repressed with imprisonment or imprisonment for two to ten years and absolute disqualification perpetual, the public official who deducts any funds or effects whose administration, perception or custody has been held due to his or her charge. An official who uses for his own benefit or a third party, works or services paid by a public administration shall be punished with the same penalty."

Brazilian Penal Code:

Peculato
"Art. 312 - To apportion the public official of money, value or any other movable asset, public or private, of

Who has the possession due to the position, or to divert it, for own or other benefit:

Penalty - confinement, from two to twelve years, and fine.

§ 1 - The same penalty applies if the public official, although not possessing the money, value or property, subtracts it, or competes for it to be subtracted, for his own or other person's benefit, using the facility that provides the quality of employee"

Paraguayan Penal Code:

"Article 300.- Passive bribery

1° The official who requests, will be allowed to promise or accept a benefit in return for a consideration derived from a behavior characteristic of the service that he has carried out or will perform in the future, will be punished with imprisonment of up to three years or with a fine."

Uruguayan Penal Code:

"Article 153. (Peculation)

The public official who appropriates the money or personal property, that is in possession by reason of his office, belonging to the State, or to individuals, for his own or another's benefit, will be punished with one year of prison to six of penitentiary and with special disqualification from two to six years."

"From the embezzlement

Article 195.- Every public official who removes the money or other movable objects from whose collection, custody or administration is in charge by virtue of his functions, will be punished with imprisonment of three to ten years. If the harm is not serious, or if it is entirely repaired before the guilty party is brought to trial, he will be imprisoned for three to twenty-one months. "

6.1 - Crimes whose effects go beyond borders of each country member of Mercosur

In the Brazilian Penal Code, the Chapter II of TITLE XI deals with crimes against the Public Administration and in it the typification of crimes that cross Brazilian borders and affect other Mercosur member countries. Here are some examples:

"Facilitation of smuggling or misconduct (Drafting given by Law no. 8,137, of 12/27/1999)

Art. 318 - To facilitate, with violation of functional duty, the practice of contraband or misconduct (article 334):

Penalty - imprisonment, from 3 (three) to 8 (eight) years, and fine.

Smuggling or misplacement

Art. 334 Importing or exporting prohibited merchandise or deceiving, in whole or in part, the payment of duty or tax due for entry, exit or consumption of merchandise:

Penalty - imprisonment, from one to four years.

Paragraph 1 - It is incumbent on the same penalty that: (Drafting provided by Law No. 4,729, of July 14, 1965)

a) Practice cabotage navigation, except in cases permitted by law;

b) Practice a fact assimilated, in a special law, to contraband or misplacement;

(c) Sells, places on sale, holds on deposit or, in any way, uses for own or of commercial or industrial activity, merchandise of foreign origin which has been smuggled into the country or imported fraudulently or which is known to be a product of clandestine introduction into the national territory or of fraudulent importation by others;

d) Acquires, receives or hides, for their own or otherwise, in the exercise of commercial or industrial activity, goods of foreign origin, unaccompanied by legal documentation, or accompanied by documents known to be false.

Paragraph 2 - For the purposes of this article, any form of illegal or clandestine commerce of foreign goods, including that exercised in residences,

Paragraph 3 - The penalty shall apply in double, if the crime of smuggling or misconduct is practiced in air transportation.

Corruption active in international commercial transactions (Incorporated by Law 10467 of 11.6.2002)

Art. 337-B. Promise, offer or give, directly or indirectly, an undue advantage to a foreign public official, or the third person, to determine, to practice, omit or delay an official act related to the international commercial transaction:

Penalty - imprisonment, from 1 (one) to 8 (eight) years, and fine.

Single paragraph. The penalty shall be increased by 1/3 (one third) if, by virtue of the advantage or promise, the public official slows down or omits the official act, or does so in breach of a duty of service.

International cooperation in international trade (Included by Law 10467 of 11.6.2002)

Art. 337-C. Request, demand, collect or obtain for themselves or for others, directly or indirectly, an advantage or promise of advantage on the pretext of impinging on an act practiced by a foreign public official in the exercise of his functions, related to an international commercial transaction:

Penalty - imprisonment, from two (2) to five (5) years, and fine.

Single paragraph. The penalty shall be increased by half if the agent alleges or implies that the advantage is also intended for a foreign official."

Our proposal to create a supra-national jurisdiction affects any crime of an economic nature in which the active or isolated subject has moved money or public property beyond the boundaries of the injured Public Administration (taxable person of the crime), since in spite of the extra-frontier effects the crimes are either tried by the national justice system or go unpunished.

In case of occurring outside the territory of one of the member countries, they will depend on treaties of international cooperation for the extradition of the active and passive subjects, with all the inefficiency that a dispersed legislation and extensive geographical borders provide.

CHAPTER 7

Concept of Public Official in the Scope of Mercosur

Having demonstrated the full existence of symmetry in Mercosur law, we now wish to prove that the terminological concept of the term "Government employee", "government official" or "public servant" in Mercosur and in the world is invariable.

We can easily say that the concept of civil servant is universal, since it is adopted by the main international conventions, as we expose below.

7.1 - According to Inter-American Convention against Corruption (IACAC):

"Article, Definitions

For the purposes of this Convention, the following definitions shall apply:

"Public service" means any activity, temporary or permanent, remunerated or honorary, performed by an individual on behalf of the State or at the service of the State or its entities, at any of its hierarchical levels.

"Government employee", "government official" or "public servant" means any official or employee of a State or its entities, including those who have been selected, appointed or elected to perform activities or functions in the name of the State or at the service of the State at any of its hierarchical levels."

7.2 - According to United Nations Convention against Corruption [UNCRC]:

"Article 2, Definitions

For the purposes of this Convention:

(a) "Civil servant" means:

(i) Any person holding a legislative, executive, administrative or judicial post of a State Party, whether appointed or employed, permanent or temporary, remunerated or honorary, irrespective of the time of such person in office;

(ii) Any person who performs a public function, including in a public body or a public undertaking, or who performs a public service, as defined in the domestic law of the State Party and applies in the relevant sphere of order legal status of that State Party;

(iii) Any person named as a "public servant" in the domestic law of a State Party. Notwithstanding, for the purposes of some specific measures included in Chapter II of this Convention, "public servants" may be understood as meaning any person who performs a public function or provides a public service second in the domestic law of the State Party and applies in the relevant sphere of the legal system of that State Party;

(b) "Foreign public servant" means any person holding a legislative, executive, administrative or judicial position in a foreign country, already designated or inducted; and any person performing a public function for a foreign country, including a public body or a public enterprise;

(c) "Official of a public international organization" shall mean an international public official or any person that such organization has authorized to act on its behalf;"

7.3 - According to the International Legal Doctrine

The doctrinal concept has full symmetry with the international and national normative concept, as Baigun and Rivas cite it (2006: 175-176):

"a. Definición de los términos "funcionario", "funcionario comunitario" y "funcionario nacional"

En la disposición introductoria se definen los términos "funcionario", "funcionario comunitario" y "funcionario nacional".

En la letra a) del art. 1 se recoge la definición de funcionario según el Convenio explicativo; la letra a) del art. 1 abarca tres categorías de personas - funcionarios de la Comunidad, funcionarios nacionales, funcionarios nacionales de otro Estado miem- bro- para asegurar una aplicación lo más homogénea posible de las disposiciones materiales del Convenio. Estas categorías se definen por referencia a su respectivos Estatutos.

En la letra b) del art. 1 la expresión "funcionario comunitario" designa tres categorías de personas: "toda persona que tenga la condición de funcionario o agente contratado en el sentido del Estatuto de los funcionarios de las comunidades europeas o del régimen aplicable a otros agentes de éstas"; "toda persona puesta a disposición de las comunidades europeas por los Estados miembros o por cualquier organismo público o privado, que ejerza en ellas funciones equivalentes a las que ejercer, los funcionarios u otros agentes de las comunidades europeas; "los miembros de organizaciones creadas de conformidad con los Tratados constitutivos de las comunidades europeas, así como el personal de dichos organismos, en la medida en que el estatuto de los funcionarios de las comunidades europeas o el régimen aplicable a otros agentes de las mencionadas comunidades les sea aplicable". Según el Convenio explicativo este último concepto incluye a los expertos nacionales destinados en las comunidades europeas para hacer funciones equivalentes a las desempeñadas por funcionarios y otros agentes comunitarios. No están incluidos en esta definición los miembros de las instituciones comunitarias como la Comisión, el Parlamento europeo, el Tribunal de Justicia y el Tribunal de Cuentas, a los que se re ere el art. 4 del Convenio. Asimismo la última frase de la letra b) incluye al personal de los organismos creados de conformidad con el derecho comunitario (el informe explicativo hace una referencia explícita a estos organismos comprendiendo entre otros, el Banco Europeo de Inversiones, la Agencia Europea de Cooperación, la Agencia Europea de Medio ambiente, etc.).

La letra c) del art. 1 dice: se entenderá por "funcionario nacional" el funcionario o el empleado público tal y como se define el concepto en el derecho nacional del Estado miembro en que la persona que se trata tenga a los fines de la aplicación del Derecho penal de dicho Estado miembro."

7.4 - In Criminal Code of Argentina

"ARTICLE 77.- For the intelligence of the text of this code, the following rules shall be kept in mind: (...)

By the terms "public official" and "public employee", used in this code, anyone who accidentally or permanently participates in the exercise of public functions is appointed, either by popular election or by appointment of a competent authority."

7.5 - In Criminal Code of Brazil

In Brazil, there are authors and teachers who want to attribute pejorative meaning to the term "public servant", saying that the expression should be used only when the public agent is an active subject of crime.

Although there are good explanations about the better terminology being "public servants" and not "civil servants", such as those of José Cretella Junior, I, particularly, think it is only a question of whether or not the criterion of "public function" which governs the general government.

Here is the Brazilian concept of public official that we extracted from the Penal Code: 4 48

"Art. 327 - A civil servant, for criminal purposes, is considered to be a person who, although temporarily or without remuneration, holds a position, job or public function.

Paragraph 1 - It is equated to a civil servant who holds a position, job or function in a parastatal entity, and who works for a company that provides services contracted or contracted for the execution of a typical Public Administration activity.

(...)

"Foreign Public Employee

Art. 337-D. For the purposes of criminal proceedings, a foreign civil servant is considered to be a person who, although temporarily or unpaid, holds a position, job or public function in state entities or in diplomatic representations of a foreign country.

Single paragraph. A foreign public official is a person who holds a position, job or position in companies controlled directly or indirectly by the Public Power of a foreign country or in international public organizations.

7.6 - In Public Service Law of Paraguay

"LAW No 1.626, OF THE PUBLIC FUNCTION,

Article 3.- In this law, the civil servant or public employee are equivalent terms, with the same juridical scope regarding their rights and responsibilities in the exercise of the public function.

(...)

Article 4.- A public official is the person appointed by administrative act to occupy permanently a position included or foreseen in the General Budget of the Nation, where he performs tasks inherent to the function of the agency or entity of the State in which he provides his services. The work of the public official is paid and is provided in relation to dependence with the State."

7.7 - In Constitution and Penal Code of Uruguay

«Constitution

"Article 25.- When the damage has been caused by its officials, in the exercise of their functions or on the occasion of that exercise, in case of having acted with serious fault or fraud, the corresponding public body may repeat against them, which I would have paid in reparation."

Penal Code

ARTICLE 175. (Concept of public official). - For the purposes of this Code, officials are considered to be all those who hold a position or perform a paid or free, permanent or temporary function, of a legislative, administrative or judicial nature, in the State, in the Municipality or in any public entity or non-state public person."

7.8 - In Criminal Code of Venezuela

"Article 236.- For the purposes of the criminal law, public officials are considered as:

1.- All those who are invested with public functions, even if they are transitory, remunerated or free, and have as their object the service of the Republic, of any State of the Republic, Territory or Federal Dependency, Section, District or Municipality or a public establishment subject by law to guardianship of any of these entities.

2.- The agents of the public force. Assume public officials, from the point of view of the legal consequences, the judges, associates, juries, arbitrators, experts, interpreters, witnesses and prosecutors during the exercise of their functions."

In all Mercosur countries, the adopted subjective functional criterion is the used one to define who is a civil servant.

In the case of Uruguay, the relationship between the function and the official was described in a masterly way by article 59 of the Constitution, as below:

"The law shall establish the Statute of the Civil Servant on the fundamental basis that the official exists for the function and not the function for the official."

CHAPTER 8

Unification or Integration in Mercosur: What is it about?

At the outset, it must be said that the processes that exist in international forum deal with economic integration and in any process of international integration, one of the fundamental aspects is the legal one, as Rabinovich-Berkman (2006: 235) put it. However, let us agree that integration is no longer new.

The proposal that we do in this book is unification of criminal law, procedure penal and administrative-disciplinary legislation, with a creation of a Permanent Court of criminal and administrative-disciplinary jurisdiction, for prosecution and trial of crimes and acts of misconduct against public administrations of Mercosur member countries.

On the processes of economic integration, Professor Jorge Horacio Schijman, Philosofer Doctor in Law and Social Sciences, highlighted clearly the importance of integration processes for the contemporary world.

Here is an excerpt from the newspaper Conceptos - Boletín de la Universidad del Museo Social Argentino, AÑO 81 – Enero – Diciembre 2006 - Ciencias Jurídicas. – The Justice in integration processes (Page 5):

"The world of our days is experiencing with great rapidity, amplitude and depth, intense changes of sign cat iva relevance.

The social, economic, technological, educational, political and cultural changes that take place in the world demand

116

a continuous adaptation of the policies and their priorities; expanding and deepening cooperation among States.

In a world where globalization and integration processes are significant, imbue us with solid regional integration projects is an opportunity that we should not miss if we want to improve our future and that of those who will continue in this life."

The integration of nations is not a new idea. Throughout history, there are reports of not a few covenants or alliances of Nations aiming mutual aid against common enemies. Here is a Biblical account of the subject:

"Joshua 9. And it came to pass, when all the kings that were over the Jordan, and in the mountains, and in the plain, and all the coast of the great sea, before Lebanon, the Hittites, and the Amorites, the Canaanites, the Perizzites, the Hivites, and the Jebusites joined themselves together to fight against Joshua and against Israel. In addition, the inhabitants of Gibeon hearing what Joshua did with Jericho and Ai. They used cunning, and they went and became ambassadors, and carried old sackcloth on their donkeys, and bottles of wine, old, and broken, and mended; And on his feet old and mended shoes, and old garments upon him; and all the bread, which they brought into the way, was dry and moldy. In addition, they came to Joshua, and to the camp, and to Gilgal, and said unto him and to the men of Israel, We came from a land far off; do now, then, with us."

In addition, the Greeks, too, did their agreements of confederation integration:

"The feud between Athens and Sparta also began after a resounding joint victory. In 479 BCE, in the battle of Audessa, the two city-states had led the Greeks in the expulsion of the Persian invaders. Shortly afterwards, however, the mutual disaffection took over both the allies. Sparta feared the naval supremacy of Athens, which continued to lead the Greeks in the struggle to liberate the Asian city-states still under Persian rule. In the following years, Athens filled the vault with looting of the battles and extended its sphere of influence throughout the Aegean Sea, consolidating the League of Delos.

However, the Athenians also felt insecure about the Spartans. While Athens had expanded its influence by the sea, Sparta had used its disciplined army to gain supremacy within the Peloponnese peninsula in southern Greece. With the "yard" in order, what would prevent the Spartans from clamoring for more power?

(...)

Fearing a sudden attack by Sparta, the Athenians decided to erect a wall around them. The Spartans said nothing (according to Thucydides, they were "secretly bitter"). But after the wall was built, the radicals of Sparta proposed an immediate attack. They were contained after an intense debate.

The situation, however, would be further complicated. In 465 BCE, Sparta faced a slave revolt. Since all the city-states that had fought against the Persians were allies, several parts of Greece came to their aid.

Athens was no exception: he sent a group of hoplites (soldiers who wore armor). The Spartans, however, asked them to withdraw from there, carrying their "dangerous ideas" together. The fear, of course, was that the people of Sparta felt attracted to democracy. The Athenians withdrew, but they were offended. They broke up the alliance with Sparta and made a pact with the city-state of Argos, the Spartan's worst enemy."

It could be said that in ancient history, integration was sought through military power and wars of annexation of territories, but the truth is that the motives were always economic because what each nation sought was to protect and increase its own wealth by drawing the treasury from other peoples.

Luciana de Andrade Mendonça (2005: 117) says:

"Integration is the act of uniting, grouping. (...) The regionalization among nation states is also. Ideally, integration occurs when groups come to be represented by a political, economic or symbolic unit, to which they are incorporated as citizens (MAUSS, 1972; ALVAREZ, 1995). Mercosur is a macro process of regional integration among the nation states, created to face the current process of globalization that has the European Union as one of the greatest exponents.

Integration as we know it today has expanded after the First World War to create more dialogue between sovereign states. Subsequently, it acquires a economic connotation, as Dr. Schijman (2006: 6) says:

"From the sixties, we find economic integration policy actions in Latin America, such as the Economic Commission for Latin America (ECLAC) (...) With the signing of the Treaty of Asunción (Paraguay), on 26 May 1991, Argentina, Brazil, Paraguay and Uruguay constitute the Common Market of the South (Mercosur) and, with the Protocol of Ouro Preto (Brazil) of December 17, 194, update the base structure of the founding Treaty, incorporating the personality international legal framework for Mercosur."

Integration has been discussed in Mercosur, from the main modern paradigms that are the European Union and NAFTA.

Professor Rui Manoel Gens de Moura Ramos, Vice-President of the Constitutional Court of Portugal at the third meeting of the Supreme Courts of Mercosur (2007: 223-224), at a conference on "The European Judicial Experience in Strengthening Community Law" Affirmed:

"The subject I will discuss is that of European judicial experience in strengthening Community law, that is to say, the way in which the European model of integration has chosen a judicial framework in which control over the application of Community law to organs has been given which is of particular importance in the context

119

of the possible role of Mercosur, and which today has an experience which can be considered to be settled.

Yesterday, we saw that the Judicial Pillar was somewhat overlooked in the construction of Mercosul by its founding fathers. And it is a bit paradoxical, as stressed by President Nelson Jobim yesterday, that this pillar has been put aside and that today the Judiciary or elements of the Judiciary are here to underline the somewhat perverse consequences of this omission and and therefore of its non-consideration in the context of that procedure.

However, if we think about it a little, we can see that this is not so strange. In the framework of the European Union, too, the Judiciary branch, although it has been present from the beginning, was not initially perceived in its importance. Only later did the agents of the integration process come to realize this reality.

In the European Union, there was something new in this picture, which was the importance of law in the name of European integration. In addition, it can be said that, in fact, it is the first time that, within the framework of the European Continent's integration, law has emerged as a relevant factor. The European integration or the European reintegration comes from very far, in m, if not of the Roman Empire, comes from Charlemagne, at least, but was always seen like something that was inaugurated by the force.

In addition, it is only at the height of World War II that the dream of integration is reborn by others means, other forms, by the use of law. In addition, in recourse to the law, there is a clear and first notion that integration must be done through the creation of permanent and solid institutes and of rules created by legal instruments, and that the phenomenon of integration must live and be developed in the light of implementation and in compliance with those rules.

Hence, we speak of the community, of the first institution that emerged, as a whole, as a community of Right, meaning that its origin and formation not only leads to the Law, but also it is the element that presides over its development.

Therefore, the law and its application have been at the center of the integration process. In order to be so, for the application of the law to be a central factor in the evolution of that process, it imputed to create a judicial system, a system of organs that could answer for the execution and the effective application of the Community Law. It was necessary that the rules should not go unpunished, that the behavior of the various agents involved in the integration process could see the law-enforced behavior achieved.

I speak here of the various actors, because in the context of the integration process, from the beginning, it became very clear in the European system that it had to rely on the states and the bodies created by the integration process - yesterday, here, the importance of these bodies when the representative of the Mercosur Administrative Secretariat referred to the ongoing projects - with legal agents, singular economic agents, individuals and coactive people; therefore, all this involved in a concession of supranationality that allowed direct relation of the individuals with, of the economic agents and, today, of the people, in the background, the evolution of the European community system has made feel in a direction in which people of the economic organ- ism operate the citizen, who, today, has a statute such as that of the Union.

The problem that this concession of supranationality raises, within the framework of the Judiciary, is, first, the one of the citizen's access to the European jurisdiction. This is an issue, first, emphasized in its importance by the circumstance, by virtue of the mechanism also of supranationality, of the applied directly in the national sphere. In addition, when it is applied, there is a natural possibility of recourse to national courts to obtain control of the application of these rules."

On the importance of the Community jurisdictional system and its experience as a paradigm for Mercosur, said Professor Rui Manoel (2207: 225-228)

"In this set, the Community Jurisdictional System has relevant pillars, the national courts and the judicial bodies of the Member States. There is, therefore, a duality, the reality of a system which is based on the existence of own tribunals, created especially for the Community system and which must coexist with the existing national courts in the Member States' legal system.

This makes the Community Jurisdictional System turn out to be complex, and its complexity comes from the existence of distinct entities that need to be arranged and must coexist with each other. (...)

National courts are, therefore, bodies governed by common law, and are therefore competent, without reservation, for all disputes between economic agents, which are settled in accordance with the application of Community rules. That is to say, the situation mentioned by Ambassador Sérgio Amaral yesterday is commonplace in the current European framework.

There is a dispute, for example, on jurisdiction and competition within the European Union, and the courts competent to resolve it are the national courts of another country, depending on the circumstances, in the case, the litigation or the jurisdiction criteria for this purpose. Therefore, the courts of the community do not have to interfere in this framework.

With regard to the competence of the Community courts, the so-called "conferral jurisdiction", the question is somewhat different. From the outset, the powers of the community courts were left to some extent to be which raise constitutional problems within the community structure.

There is, first, an essential question, namely, the question of the violations of Community law by the Member States. These questions somehow underline the will of the state to at least enforce the standards to which it has bound itself. There is also the possibility - just mentioned - of individuals demanding compliance at the national level; the possibility of a procedure initiated, in principle, by the commission, as a body that ensures compliance with the treaties.

The committee has the possibility of initiating a judicial procedure in the middle of an administrative procedure, which may lead to the condemnation of States, which is, say, frequent and has not given rise to special problems. Moreover, the field of choice of these convictions is the enforcement of EU directives in cases where there is a need to internalize the rules of the European Union. States are often condemned. This condemnation only had as consequence the fact that they came to execute the rule later. Subsequently, Community case law gave rise to important principles such as the responsibility of the Member States for breaches of Community law and therefore the consequences that such relationships may have on individuals.

Nowadays, it is also possible in a national court to ask the State to assume responsibility for the omission of that State in the enforcement of a directive - to use the language of Mercosur, I would say in the internalization of an act of the Mercosul.

Of course, within the framework of the European Union, one can speak of omission, because there is a deadline for the implementation of the directives, so the State has an obligation to exhaust it within a certain period; within that period, is constituted in a situation of violation. Thus, in certain circumstances, the damage which the individual may suffer as a result of that omission by the State - and we have heard a number of situations which may be said yesterday - are likely, in the light of Community expenditure, to constitute the offending State in a obligation to indemnify. (...)

This has been one of the ways that the community experience has used to solve the problem, but there is another one that I also believe should be mentioned in this exhibition, as something that may come also to take place within the Mercosur framework. It is that, in essence, the division of powers between the courts means this: if there is an act that is of the community, it has to be attacked in the community court; if there is an act which is, even under Community law, carried out by a national legal entity, then that act is attacked before the national courts."

On the relations of national judicial bodies with Community Courts and any preliminary questions that may arise, Professor Ricardo Alonso Garcia (Professor at the Faculty of Law of the Universidad Complutense de Madrid and Director of the European Institute of regional integration) also speaking at the Forum of Supreme Courts, states (2007: 237-239):

"The fathers of the Treaty of the European Union decided to leave it up to the member states, for each member state to decide freely whether or not to accept the preliminary question. And if the question is accepted, the State in question has to present a formal declaration stating that the judges and courts of its State are going to raise the preliminary questions that arise in that framework of space of security, freedom and justice.

Well, I already advance, even allowing States to admit the question and others who do not admit the question, what is very clear is that the interpretations that marks the Court of Justice in that common space, which is why it is common, of security and justice, bind all contracting parties. That is, not only those States that have accepted the preliminary ruling mechanism, but also those that have not accepted it. And I close the parenthesis. I insist on that, I will speak again at the end of the intervention, when referring to the advisory opinion in the field of Mercosur."

Insofar we advance sometimes we involute in discussing questions for what we already know the solutions. Of course the preliminary questions must be discussed in the internal legal systems and, at the end, a commom resolution must be presented to entire body of Mercosur, without any offense to the sovereingnty of each country.

The unification of the criminal, procedural penal and administrative-law will take time and hard work, but we must focus on the positive results for the Mercosur community and for other blocs in the world that could posibly absorv the example.

The end, by itself, deserves the Nations effort, because there is no doubt that as much we combat corruption with public funds, muche more money there will be in public treasury for the well being of the poeples.

FINAL CONSIDERATIONS

The question we raise throughout this book is:

The unification of criminal, procedural penal and administrative-disciplinary legislation of crimes and acts of improbity that go beyond the borders of a Mercosur country can contribute to reducing corruption?

We delimit the theme in the following thematic area:

1– Public Law: International Law. Criminal Law. Criminal Procedural Law. Administrative law. Administrative Procedural Law.
2– Political Science: Democratic Regime. Threat to Democracy.

We have proposed the main and secondary problems in the following order:

Main problem: Corruption with public funds is a threat to the democratic regime, since it prevents the state from playing its role of provider of the common good.

We have shown that there is legislation in each member country of Mercosur to combat corruption, but this legislation is designed with an internal perspective and that crimes and acts of administrative improbity that cross borders have practically the same objective and subjective elements of conduct.

These facts and all proven symmetries allows the unification the legislation we have spoke about.

The problem, therefore, lies in facts such as:

-   Disperse Criminal legislation, which can be consolidated.
-   Disperse Criminal Procedural Legislation.
-   Disperse Administrative-disciplinary Legislation.
-   Disperse Procedural Administrative-disciplinary Legislation.
-   National Judicial branches without competence to prosecute perpetrators of crimes and acts of improbity whose effects are extra-frontier.

We try not to neglect related problems, such as:

-   National sovereignty;
-   The competence of the national judiciary to deal with cases of corruption that go beyond their borders, given the reserve of each national sovereignty;
-   The possibility of considering acts of corruption against the Public Administrations of Mercosur and the world as crimes against humanity, since the diversion of public goods, money and income amounts to several genocides per day, since it kills ethnic groups of hunger in the Mercosur and in the world, according to data of international organizations reproduced in this work.

At the end, we conclude:

1– There are criminal, procedural penal and administrative-disciplinary legislation to combat corruption within the framework of each Mercosur member country.

2– That criminal, procedural penal and administrative-disciplinary laws to combat corruption within each Mercosur country are dispersed, that is, they are not properly consolidated.

3– That there is full symmetry between the criminal, procedural penal and administrative-disciplinary legislation to combat corruption within each Mercosur member country.

4– That the proven symmetry allows the unification of the criminal, procedural penal and administrative-disciplinary legislation to combat corruption within each Mercosur member country.

5– That the proven constitutional symmetry between the members of Mercosur allows the creation of a Permanent Court with criminal and administrative-disciplinary jurisdiction as supranational body.

6– That the creation of a tribunal with criminal and administrative-disciplinary jurisdiction as a supranational body in Mercosur can be done by means of a treaty;

7– That the creation of a tribunal with permanent criminal and administrative-disciplinary jurisdiction in Mercosur can contribute to a significant reduction in corruption by giving legally permition to each countru to install the *persecution criminis* and the *jus puniendi* to prosecution authors of crimes and acts of improbity against the Mercosur Public Administrations.

8– There is the Italian system as a paradigm of Administrative Justice with one law one jurisdictio.

9– There is little point in elevating acts of corruption and improbity against Public Administrations to the category of heinous crimes, if impunity is not annihilated.

10– Acts of corruption against the Mercosul and world Public Administrations should be considered crimes against humanity, according to the phatic and political-juridical foundations that we put in book 4 of this Encyclopedia.

Identifying problems and proposing solutions is not the most difficult task of life. The biggest challenge is to find people who have the courage to turn words and good thoughts into actions to change their surroundings.

A father worked in his home office. His five-year-old son interrupted him at all times, wanting to play with him. The father picked up on the desk, a map of the world, tore into several pieces and told the son that if he fixed the "world", he would stop working to play with him. A few minutes later, the son returned with the map of the world repaired and the father, surprised, asked how he had managed to fix the "world" so quickly. The son said he looked and saw that behind the world was the drawing of a man. He repaired man and the world was repaired. The father stopped working and played with his son.

   We can build a better world with more Ethics in our relationships. A world with less corruption. We can do it! I am sure that we can do it!

BIBLIOGRAPHY

AUGUSTINE, Saint. Cones. Translation of J. Oliveira Santos, S.J, Ambrósio de Pina, S.J. São Paulo: New culture, 2000. (The thinkers).

ALBISTUR, Emilio A. La corrupción como pecado social, generadora de estructuras de pecado. Centro de investigación y acción social, Argentina, Año XLV, N. 458, p. 531-533, nov. 1996.

ALCAIN, Eduardo Morón. Cuestiones jus losó cas en La Alemania de posguerra: su actualidad. Buenos Aires: Abeledo-Perrot, 1998.

ALCALDE, Carmen. La losofía. 1. ed. España: Bruguera, S.A., 1972. (SI NO).

Alertan por omisión en noti cación de hepatitis: Uruguay. Sin datos locales porque médicos no informan. EL país, Montevideo, Ciudades- B3, Domingo 17 de mayo de 2009.

ANDRIASOLA, Gabriel. Delitos de corrupción pública: análisis de la ley 17.060 de 23 de diciembre de 1998. Montevideo: Del foro S.R.L, 1999. (Monografías jurídicas 4).

ANGELL, Norman. The great illusion. Translation by Sérgio Bath. 1. ed. São Paulo: University of Brasilia, 2002. (IPRI Classics).

ARÉVALOS, Evelio Fernández. Órganos constitucionales del Estado: poder leg- islativo, poder ejecutivo, poder judicial, órganos constitucionales extrapoderes. Paraguay: Intercontinental, 2003.

ARGENTINA. (1853). Constitución de la República Argentina: sancionada el 1° de mayo de 1853, reformada y concordada por la convencion nacional ad hoc el 25 de septiembre de 1860 y con las reformas de las convenciones de 1866, 1898, 1957 y 1994. Disponível em:< http://www.senado.gov.ar/web/interes/con- stitucion/preambulo.php.> Acesso em: 26.04.2011.

ARGENTINA. Codigo de etica de la funcion pública. Decreto 41/27-ene- 1999, Publicada en el Boletín O cial del 03-feb-1999. Número: 29077. Página: 5. Disponível em:< http://www.infoleg.gov.ar> Acesso em: 27.04.2011.

ARGENTINA. Codigo penal. Ley 11179/30-sep-1921, Publicada en el Boletín O cial del 03-nov-1921, Número: 8300 Página: 1. Disponível em:< http:// www.infoleg.gov.ar> Acesso em: 27.04.2011.

ARGENTINA. Codigo procesal penal. Ley 23984/21-ago-1991, Publicada en el Boletín O cial del 09-sep-1991. Número: 27215. Disponível em:< http:// www.infoleg.gov.ar> Acesso em: 27.04.2011.

ARGENTINA. Ley 26.388/ 4 de junio del 2008 (promulgada de hecho el 24 de junio de 2008). Delitos de cuello Blanco. Disponível em: < http:// www.jgm.gov. ar> Acesso em: 27.04.2011.

ARGENTINA. Ley N° 189. Codigo contencioso administrativo y tributario de la C.A.B.A. (Boletín O cial No 722- Legislatura de la Ciudad Autónoma de Buenos Aires) Disponível em:< http://boletino cial.buenosaires.gob.ar> Acesso em: 27.04.2011.

ARGENTINA. LEY No 2303/07 - Se aprueba el código procesal penal de la ciu- dad autónoma de Buenos Aires. Disponível em:< http://www. buenosaires.gov. ar> Acesso em: 27.04.2011.

ARGENTINA. LEY No 451/00 - Aprueba texto del anexo I, como régimen de faltas de la ciudad de Buenos Aires. Sustituye denominación del capítulo IV del libro II, y del art. 47 del código contravencional, B.O. N° 405. EN EL anexo II deroga ordenanzas, leyes, decretos y resoluciones normas. Disponível em:< http://www.buenosaires.gov.ar> Acesso em: 27.04.2011.

ASOCIACION DE MAGISTRADOS DEL URUGUAY, abril 1998 Montevideo. El poder judicial frente a la corrupción. Montevideo: Liventa papelex S.R.L, 1998.

ARTANA, Daniel. Los costos económicos de la corrupción. Idea, Argentina, p. 91-92, ago. 1998.

Autoridades de las clínicas cerraron la emergencia por falta de recursos: traslados. Los pacientes son derivados hacia otros centros. EL país, Montevideo, Nacional – A5, Domingo 17 de mayo de 2009.

BACON, Francis. Novum organum ou verdadeiras indicações acerca da in- terpretação da natureza. Tradução e notas de José Aluysio Reis de Andrade. São Paulo: Nova cultura, 2000. (Os pensadores).

BAIGUN, David; RIVAS, Nicolás García (dir.). Delincuencia económica y corrupción. 1. ed. Buenos Aires: Ediar, 2006.

BAKUNIN, Michael Alexandrovich. Textos anarquistas. Tradução de Zilá Bernd. Seleção e notas Daniel Guérin. Porto Alegre: L&PM, 2006. (Coleção L&PM Pocket).

BARATTA, Alessandro Principles of minimum criminal law: for a theory of human rights as the object and limit of criminal law. Translation by Francisco Bissoli Filho. Published in the journal "Criminal doctrine n. 10-40. Buenos Aires: Depalma, 1987. Santa Catarina, 2003.

BARBOZA, Julio. Derecho Internacional Público. Buenos Aires: Zavalia,1999. BARRIO, Javier Delgado; VIGO, Rodolfo L. Sobre os princípios jurídicos. Buenos Aires: Abeledo-Perrot. 1998
[Links] Principles of minimum criminal law: for a theory of human rights as the object and limit of criminal law. Translation by Francisco Bissoli Filho. Published in the journal "Criminal doctrine n. 10-40. Buenos Aires: Depalma, 1987. Santa Catarina, 2003.

BERLINGER, Giovanni; BOTTLE, Volnei. The human market: a bioethical study of the buying and selling of body parts. Translation by Isabel Regina Augusto. Brasília: University of Brasília, 1996.

Biblia. Espanhol. Santa Biblia. Versión de Casiodoro de Reina. Madrid: Socie- dad bíblica, 1995.

BRAZIL. UN. Board of control of financial activities. Money laundering: a worldwide problem. Brasília: UNDCP, 1999.

BOBBIO, Norberto. Theory of legal order. Translated by Maria Celeste Cordeiro Leite dos Santos. 10. ed. Brasília: University of Brasília, 1999.

BRAZIL. Federal Court of Justice. Meetings of supreme courts: challenges and perspectives in the process of integration of mercosul. Brasília: Supreme Courts Forum, 2007.

CALDWELL, Taylor. Um pilar de ferro. Tradução de Luzia Machado da Costa. Rio de Janeiro: Distribuidora Record de serviços de imprensa S.A., 1965.

CARBONELL, Miguel; SALAZAR, Pedro (eds.). Garantismo: estudios sobre el pensamiento jurídico de Luigi Ferrajoli. Madrid: Trota, 2005. (colección estruc- turas y procesos serie derecho).

CASTRO, Anna Maria; DIAS, Edmundo F. Introduction to sociological thinking. 4. ed. Rio de Janeiro: Eldorado, 1976.

CATENACCI, Imerio Jorge. Introducción al derecho: teoría general. Argumentación razonamiento jurídico. 1. ed. Buenos Aires: Astrea, 2006. V. 1. Re- impresión. (Colección mayor Filosofía y derecho v. 7).

CHAUI, Marilena. What is ideology. 26. ed. São Paulo: Editora brasiliense, 1988. (First 13 steps).

CHOMSKY, Noam. Reasons for status. Translated by Vera Ribeiro. Rio de Janeiro: Record, 2008.

CHURCHILL, Winston S. Memories of the Second World War. Translated by Vera Ribeiro. 2. ed. Rio de Janeiro: New Frontier, 1995. v. 7. Printing.

CICERÓN. Los Oficios. Traducción Manuel de Valbuena. Madrid: Espasa. (Grandes clásicos universales).

CINCUNEGUI, Juan Bautista; CINCUNEGUI, Juan de Dios. La corrupción y los factores de poder. 1. ed. Argentina: Fundación Argentina de planeamiento, 1996.

COLEGIO DE CONTADORES Y ECONOMISTAS DEL URUGUAY. "Cambios en la administración nanciera gubernamental". Montevideo: colegio de contadores y economistas del Uruguay. 1999.

COMISSIÓN DE SEGUIMENTO DEL CUMPLIMIENTO DE LA CONVEN- CIÓN INTERAMERICANA CONTRA LA CORRUPCIÓN. Colegio público de abogados de la capital federal. Buenos Aires, 2002.

COMISIÓN ECONÓMICA PARA AMÉRICA LATINA Y EL CARIBE. Balance preliminar de las economías de América latia y el Carbe. Chile: Naciones unidas, 2008.

COMISIÓN ECONÓMICA PARA AMÉRICA LATINA Y EL CARIBE. Estu- dio económico de América latina y el Caribe: política macroeconómica y volatilidad. Chile: Naciones unidas, 2008.

COMTE, Auguste. Curso de loso a positiva. Traducción de Carmen Lessin- ing. 1. Ed. Buenos Aires: Need, 2004. (Ediciones libertador).

CONSEJO DE LA MAGISTRATURA PODER JUDICIAL DE LA CIUDAD DE BUENOS AIRES. La plani cación estratégica en la justicia de la ciudad de Bue- nos Aires. Argentina: Geudeba, 2008.

CONVENCIÓN DE NACIONES UNIDAS CONTRA LA CORRUPCIÓN : Nuevos paradigmas para la prevención y combate de la corrupción en el esce- nario global. 1. ed. Buenos Aires: O cina anticorrupción. Ministerio de Justicia y Derechos Humanos, 2004.

Corrupción y democracia en la argentina: La interpretación de los estudiantes uni- versitarios. Revista Argentina de sociología. Argentina, año 3, N°4, p. 9-31, 2005.

COSTA, José Armando. Legal outline of administrative improbity. Brasília: Legal Brasília, 2000.

COULANGES, Fustel de. The ancient city: studies on worship, law, institutions of Greece and Rome. Translation by Jonas Camargo Leite and Eduardo Fonseca. São Paulo: Hemus, 1975.

CRETELLA JUNIOR, José. Course of Roman law. 1. ed. Rio de Janeiro: forensic, 1968.

CHRISTIAN, Fortini. et al. (Org.). Public policies: possibilities and limits. Belo Horizonte: Forum, 2008.

CROCE, Benedetto. et al. Declarations of rights. Brasília: Rondon Project Foundation, 1988.

DARWIN, Charles. El origen de las espécies. 1. ed. Buenos Aires: centro editor de cultura, 2006.

DELMAS-MARTY, Mireille. Three challenges for a world right. Translation and afterword of Fauzi Hassan Choukr. Rio de Janeiro: Lumen Juris, 2003.

DEPARTMENT OF PROTECTION AND ECONOMIC DEFENSE OF THE SECRETARY OF ECONOMIC LAW OF THE MINISTRY OF JUSTICE. Combo to cartels and leniency programs. Brasília: publication o cial, 2008. (SDE / DPDE 01/2008).

DESCARTES. Discourse of method, the passions of the soul, meditations. São Paulo: New culture, 2000. (The thinkers).

DONZELE, Patrícia F. L. Aspects of Sovereignty in International Law: Addresses the internal and external aspects of sovereignty, analyzing the subsistence of same in the process of integration verified in the international scope. Available at: <http://www.direitonet.com.br/artigos/exibir/1496/Aspectos-de- Sovereignty-in-Law-International>. Accessed on: 03.06.2011.

ECO, Umberto. Como se hace una tesis: técnicas y procedimientos de investigación, estudio y escritura. Barcelona: Editora Gedisa, S.A., 1988.

EL PODER JUDICIAL ANTE LA CORRUPCIÓN. Cuaderno No 2, 2004, Montevideo. ¿Qué justicia queremos? Uruguay: asociación de funcionarios judiciales del Uruguay, 2004. 32 p.

ENGELS, Friedrich. The origin of the family, the private property and the State. Translation Ciro Mioranza. São Paulo: Scale. (Great works of universal thought - 2).

ETKIN, Jorge Ricardo. La doble moral de las organizaciones: los sistemas per- versos y La corrupción institucionalizada. España: McGRAW-HILL, 1993. p. 266.

FERMÍN, Claudio. 100 razones para salir de Chávez. Venezuela: Democracia y periodismo, 2004.

FERNANDES, A.; GAVEGLIO, S.(comp.). Globalización, integración, Mercosur y desarrollo local. 1. ed. Argentina: Homo Sapiens Ediciones, 2000.

FORO UNIÓN EUROPEA, AMÉRICA LATINA Y EL CARIBE LAS POLÍTICAS FISCALES EN TIEMPOS DE CRISIS: VOLATILIDAD, COHESIÓN SOCIAL Y ECONOMÍA POLÍTICA DE LAS REFORMAS. 2009, Montevideo. El papel de la política tributaria frente a la crisis global: consecuencias y perspectivas. Montevideo: Naciones unidas, 2009. 48p.

FORO UNIÓN EUROPEA, AMÉRICA LATINA Y EL CARIBE LAS POLÍTI- CAS FISCALES EN TIEMPOS DE CRISIS: VOLATILIDAD, COHESIÓN SO- CIAL Y ECONOMÍA POLÍTICA DE LAS REFORMAS. 2009, Montevideo. Crisis, volatilidad, ciclo y política scal en América latina. Montevideo: Naciones unidas, 2009. 44 p.

GALES CASA CAMBIARIA LESPAN S. A. Manual de prevención de lavado de activos. Montevideo- Uruguay: Gales casa cambiaria lespan S. A., 2004. 119 p.

GALVÃO, Eduardo Rodrigues. Study of Brazilian problems. 3. ed. Brasília: Federal Senate, Graphic Center, 1985.

GILES, omas Ransom. History of education. São Paulo: EPU, 1987.
GOMÁ, Javier. Public Exemplarity. 2. Ed. Madrid: Taurus thought, 2009.

GOMES, Luís Roberto. The public ministry and the control of administrative omission: the control of the State Omission in Environmental Law. 1. ed. Rio de Janeiro: University Forensics, 2003.

GRONDONA, Mariano. La corrupción. 3. ed. Argentina: Editorial planeta Argentina, 1993.

GUEDES, Je erson Cárus; SOUZA, Luciane Moessa (coord.). State Advocacy: institutional issues for the construction of a State of justice: studies in Homage to Diogo de Figueiredo Moreira Neto and José Antônio Dias Toffoli. Belo Horizonte: Forum, 2009.

HEIDEMANN, Francisco; SALM, José Francisco (Org.). Public policies and development: epistemological bases and models of analysis. 2. ed. Brasília: University of Brasilia, 2010.

HESPANHA, António Manuel. Cultura jurídica européia: síntese de um milênio. Florianópolis: Fundação Boiteux, 2005.

HOMERO. The Odyssey. Translation and adaptation Fernando C. de Araújo Gomes. São Paulo: Scale. (Master thinkers).

HUM AND. São Paulo: New culture, 2000. (The thinkers).

JACKSON, Philip W., et al. La vida moral en la escuela. Traducción de Glória Vitale. Buenos Aires: Amorrortu, 2003.

JIMÉNEZ, Juan Pablo; PODESTÁ, Andrea. Inversión, incentivos scales y gastos tributarios en América latina. Santiago de Chile: Naciones Unidas, 2009. (Serie macroeconomía del desarrollo).

JUNTA ASESORA EN MATERIA ECONÓMICO FINANCEIRA DEL ES- TADO. Ética y función pública. 1. ed. Montevideo: Tarma, 2008. 60 p. (Serie: "manuales de capacitación" no 1).

JUNTA ASESORA EN MATERIA ECONÓMICO FINANCEIRA DEL ESTA- DO. Normas de conduta en la función pública. Montevideo: Tarma, 2007.

KAFKA, Franz. Consideraciones acerca del pecado: cuadernos en octava. Buenos Aires: Ediciones libertador, 2004. (Edición especial).

KAFKA, Franz. The process. São Paulo: Martin Claret, 2000. (The masterpiece of each author).

KANT, Immanuel. Critique of pure reason. Translation by Valerio Rohden and Udo Baldur Moosburger. São Paulo: New culture, 2000. (The thinkers).

KANENGUISER, Nartín. El n de La ilusión: Argentina 2001·2011 crisis, re- construcción y declive. 1. ed. Buenos Aires: Edhasa, 2011.

KLUG, Ulrich. Lógica jurídica. Traducción de J. C Gardella. Bogotá: Temis, 2004. v. 2. Reimpresión

KNELLER, George F. Science as a human activity. Translation by Antonio José de Souza. Rio de Janeiro: Zahar, 1980.

LA LUCHA MUNDIAL CONTRA LA CORRUPCIÓN. Foro Politico: Revista del Instituto de Ciencias Politicas. v.XVI Buenos Aires: Universidad del Museo Social Argentino, Marzo 1996. p. 76-81.

LANDES, David S. Wealth and the poverty of nations: why some are so rich and others so poor. 2. ed. Translation Álvaro Cabra. Rio de Janeiro: Campus, 1998.

LENAY, Charles. La evolución: de La bactéria al hombre. Traducción y adaptación Pilar Martinez. Barcelona: RBA, 1994. (Conocer la ciencia).

LEVI, José Fernando Casañas. Legislación penal Paraguaya: código penal concordado, código procesal penal concordado, leyes complementares, acordadas y resoluciones de la corte suprema de justicia, resoluciones del ministerios público, índice alfabético. Paraguay: Intercontinental, 2006. (legislación Paraguaya edición 2006).

LOCKE, John. Essay on human understanding. Translation of Anoie Aiex. São Paulo: New culture, 2000. (The thinkers).

LOCKE, John. Second Treatise about Government. Translated by Alex Marins. São Paulo: Martin Claret, 2002. (The masterpiece of each author)

LONG, Kim. E almanac of political corruption, scandals & dirty politics. New York: Delacorte press, 2007.

MAHIQUES, Carlos Alberto (Dir.). El derecho penal: doctrina y jurisprudencia. Buenos Aires: El derecho, 2005. p. 6

MAIRAL, Héctor A., Las raíces legales de la corrupción: o de cómo el derecho público fomenta la corrupción en lugar de combatirla. 1. ed. Argentina: Ediciones Rap S.A, 2007.

MALMESBURY, Omas Hobbes. Leviathan or matter, form and power of an ecclesiastical and civil State. Translation by João Paulo Monteiro and Maria Beatriz Nizza da Silva. São Paulo: New culture, 2000. (The thinkers).

MANCUSO, Hugo R. Metodología de La investigación em ciências sociales: lineamientos teóricos y prácticos de semioepistemología. 1. ed. Buenos Aires: Paidós, 2006. 3. v. Reimpresión.

MANCUSO, Rodolfo de Camargo. Public civil action: in defense of the environment, cultural heritage and consumers. 8. ed. Brazil: Journal of the Courts, 2002.

MANFRONI, Carlos A. La convención interamericana contra la corrupción. 2. Ed. Argentina: Abeledo-Perrot, 2001.

MANFRONI, Carlos A. Soborno transnacional. 1. Ed. Argentina: Abeledo-Perrot, 1998.

Manual on monitoring of alternative penalties and measures. Brazil: pan er Graphic, 2002.

MARTINO, Antonio A. Etica y democracia. Foro Politico: Revista del Instituto de Ciencias Politicas. v.XII. Buenos Aires: Universidad del Museo Social Argen- tino, Diciembre 1994. p. 7-10.

MENDIETA, Manuel Villoria. Ética pública y corrupción: curso de ética ad- ministrativa. 1. ed. Madrid: Editorial Tecnos grupo Anaya S.A., 2000.

MENY, Yves; THOENIG, Jean-Claude. Las políticas públicas. Versión Española Francisco Morata. Traducción de Salvador Del Carril. 1. ed. Barcelona: Ariel ciencia política, 1992.

MINISTERIO DE JUSTICIA Y DERECHOS HUMANOS: balance de gestion; o cina anticorrupcion. Argentina, 2000. p. 49

MINISTERIO FEDERAL DE COOPERACIÓN ECONOMICA Y DESARROL- LO. Carpeta de información: la cooperación alemana para el desarrollo con América latina y el Caribe. Berlim, 2005.

MONTESQUIEU. Of the spirit of the laws. v. 1. São Paulo: New culture, 2000. (The thinkers).

MONTI, Víctor Manuel. Corrupción, gobierno y democracia. Ricardo G. Her- rera (Col) 1. Ed. Santiago del Estero: UNCa, 1999.

MOREIRA NETO, Diogo de Figueredo. Four paradigms of postmodern administrative law: legitimacy, nality, and science, results. Belo Horizonte: Forum, 2008.

MORO, Tomas. *Utopia*. Traducción María Guillermina Nicolini. Buenos Aires: editorial La Página S.A. editorial Losada S.A. 2003.

NEUMANN, Ulfried. La pretensión de verdad en el derecho: y três ensayos so- bre Radbruch. Traducción Mauricio Hernández. 1. ed. Colombia: Universidad externado de Colombia, 2006. (Serie de teoria jurídica y loso a Del derecho n 38).

NIETZSCHE, Friedrich. Así habló Zaratustra. Traducción por J. C García Bor- rón. 1. ed. Buenos Aires: Centro editor de cultura, 2007.

NIETZSCHE, Friedrich. La genealogía de la moral. Traducción por Sergio Al- bano. 1. ed. Buenos Aires: Gradifco, 2007. (Pensadores universales).

NIETZSCHE, Friedrich. Más allá del bien y del mal. Traducción por Sergio Albano. 1. ed. Caseros: Gradifco, 2007. (Pensadores universales).

NINO, Carlos Santiago. Ética y derechos humanos: un ensayo de fundament- ación. 2. ed. Buenos Aires: Astrea, 2007. V. 2. Reimpresión. (Colección mayor Filosofía y derecho v. 15).

NÚÑEZ, José Ariel. Manual de auditoría gubernamental: control democrático contra La corrupción y el despilfarro. Buenos Aires: Ediciones Rap, 2006.

OLIVÉ, Juan Carlos Ferré. Et al. Blanqueo de dinero y corrupción en el sistema bancario: delitos nancieros, fraude y corrupción en Europa. V. II. España: Universidad de salamanca, 2002.

OLIVEIRA, Harrison. Reflections on the misery of the northeast. Paraíba: "The union" Cia. Publisher, 1984.

OLIVEIRA, Odete Maria. Prison: a social paradox. 3. ed. Santa Catarina: Ed. Da UFSC, 2003.

OLIVEIRA, Roberto Cardoso; BAINES, Stephen G. (Org.). Nationality and ethnicity at borders. Brasília: University of Brasília, 2005. (Americas Collection).

PALACIO, Ernesto. Catilina: una revolución contra la plutocracia en Roma. Buenos Aires: Abeledo-Perrot, 1998.

THE PALOMBARA, Joseph. Politics within the nations. Brasília: University of Brasília, 1982. (Political thought 60).

PARAGUAY. Constitución (1992). Constitución de la república del Paraguay: promulgación 16 de agosto de 1992. Elaborado por Horacio Antonio pettit. Para- guay: Intercontinental, 2008. (tomo IV libro noveno).

PASSET, René. The neoliberal illusion. Translation by Clóvis Marques. Rio de Janeiro: Record, 2002.

PATEL, Ketan J. The master of strategy: power, purpose and principle. Translation by Ricardo Doninelli. Rio de Janeiro: Bestseller, 2007.

PEGORARO, Juan S. La corrupción como cuestión social y como cuestión penal. Delito y society, Buenos Aires, Year 8, n.13, p. 6-32, 1999.

PEREIRA JUNIOR, Jessé Torres. The right to defense in the 1998: Constitution: the administrative procedure and the accused in general. Rio de Janeiro: Renovar, 1991.

PORTO, Maria Stela Grossi; DWYER, Tom (Org.). Sociology and reality: social research in the 21st century. Brasília: University of Brasília, 2006.

PRITZL, Rupert: Corrupción y Rentismo en América Latina. Buenos Aires: Ciedla, Fundación Honrad Adenauer, 2000.

PROGRAMA DE COOPERACIÓN CEPAL- GTZ. Memoria anual marzo 2007- marzo 2008. Santiago de Chile: Naciones unidas, 2007-2008.

PUERTO, Carlos Gonzalez del; MÓDICA, Yeny Villalba y Gisela Di (Comp.).

Compilación legislativa en materia de prevención y lucha contra la corrup- ción. Paraguay: Publicación del instituto de estudios en ciencias penales y so- ciales del Paraguay (Inecip), 2004.

QUINTA CUMBRE DE LAS AMERICAS. 5. 2009, Puerto España. La reacción de los gobiernos de las Américas frente a la crisis internacional:

una present- ación sintética de las medidas de política anunciadas hasta el 31 de marzo de 2009. Santiago de Chile: Naciones unidas, 2009. 57 p.

RABINOVICH – BERKMAN, Ricardo David. Derechos humanos: uma introducción a su naturaleza y a su historia. 1. ed. Buenos Aires: Quorum, 2007.

RABINOVICH – BERKMAN, Ricardo David. Principios generales del derecho latinoamericano. Buenos Aires: Astrea, 2006.

RABINOVICH – BERKMAN, Ricardo David. Un viaje por la historia del derecho. 1. ed. Buenos Aires: Quorum, 2007.

REIS, Claudio Araujo. Unity & Liberty: The Individual According to Jean-Jacques Rousseau. Brasília: Editora universidade de Brasília: Finatec, 2005.

CIA REPORT: how will the world be in 2010. Translation by Claudio Blanc and Marly Netto Peres. São Paulo: Ediouro, 2006.

REPUBLICA DEL PARAGUAY. Manual de procedimientos estadísticas penales antecedentes judiciales. Paraguay, 2007.

REPÚBLICA ORIENTAL DEL URUGUAY. Ley de fortalecimiento del sistema de prevención y control del lavado de activos y nanciación del terrorismo: ley no 17.835 del 23/09/004. Uruguay: Direccion nacional de impresiones y publicaciones o ciales. 2004.

RIMONDI, Jorge Luis. Cali cación legal de los actos de corrupción en La administración pública. 1. ed. Buenos Aires: Ad- Hoc, 2005.

ROJAS, Ricardo M. Algunas consideraciones co-políticas en torno al problema de la corrupción. Foro Politico: Revista del Instituto de Ciencias Politicas. v. VII. Buenos Aires: Universidad del Museo Social Argentino, Abril 1993. p. 61-82.

RUGNITZ, José. La polibanda. Montevideo: La republica, 2002. (Caso clave: temas de investigación de la república).

SANTOS, Jerônimo Jesus. Conduct adjustment Term. 1. ed. Rio de Janeiro: Publisher and legal bookstore of Rio de Janeiro, 2005.

SAMPAIO, Plínio Arruda. How to fight corruption. São Paulo: Paulus, 2009.

SCHIJMAN, JORGE HORACIO. La Justicia en los procesos de integración. *Conceptos - Boletín de la Universidad del Museo Social Argentino,* Argentina, Ciencias Jurídicas, p. 5, AÑO 81 – Enero – Diciembre 2006.

SCHMITT, Carl. Political theology. Translation by Elisete Antoniuk. Belo Horizonte: Del Rey, 2006.

SCHOPENHAUER, Arthur. Ensayo sobre al libre albedrío: la libertad. Traducción por Sergio Albano. Buenos Aires: Gradifco, 2006. (Pensadores universales).

SIGMUND, Freud. Complete works. Translation by Luis Lopez. v. 2. Madrid: new library Madrid, 1968.

SILVA, Nelson Lehmann. The civil religion of the modern state. Brasília: esaurus, 1985.

SKINNER, Quentin. The foundations of modern political thought. Translation Renato Janine Ribeiro and Laura Texeira Motta. São Paulo: Companhia das letras, 2006. v. 4. Reprint.

SMITH, Adam. Vida, pensamiento y obra. España (colección grandes pensa dores).1997.

SOUZA, Jessé (org.). Democracy today: new to democratic contemporary theory. 1. ed. Brazil: University of Brasília, 2001.

SPINOZA, Baruch de. Ethics: demonstrated in the manner of geometers. São Paulo: Martin Claret, 2002. (The masterpiece of each author)

SUPIOT, Alain. Homo juridicus: ensayo sobre La función antropológica Del derecho. Traducción de Silvio Mattoni. 1. ed. Buenos Aires: Siglo veintiuno edi- tores, 2007 (Sociología y política).

Teixeira, João Gabriel Lima (coord.). The construction of citizenship. Brasília: University of Brasilia, 1986.

TOCQUEVILLE, Alexis de. La democracia en América. Traducción de Luis R. Cuéllar. 2. Ed. México: Fondo de Cultura Económica, 1957.13.v. Reimpresión.

TODARELLO, Guillermo Ariel. Corrupción administrativa y enriquecimiento ilícito. 1. ed. Buenos Aires: Del Puerto, 2008.

TRIGUEIRO, André. Sustainable world 2: new directions for a planet in crisis. São Paulo: Globo, 2012

TRINDADE, Antônio Augusto Cançado. The exhaustion of domestic remedies in international law. 2. Ed. Brasília: publisher of Brasília, 1997.

VAINER, Ari, et al. Managing scal responsible municipal simple: annual budget law manual elaboration. Brasília: Area of communication and culture-executive marketing management, 2001.

VAINER, Ari, et al. Management scal responsible simple municipal: pluri-annual plan manual elaboration. Brasília: Area of communication and culture-executive marketing management, 2001.

VAINER, Ari, et al. Managing scal responsible municipal simple: budget directives budget manual drafting. Brasília: Area of communication and culture-executive marketing management, 2001.

VÁZQUEZ, Mariana Malet. La corrupción en la administración pública: aproximación a la ley no 17.060 normas referidas al uso indebido del poder público. Montevideo: Carlos Alvarez. 1999.

VIDAL, J. W. Bautista. From servile state to sovereign nation: solidarity civilization of the tropics. Petrópolis: Vozes, 1987.

VIGO, Rodolfo Luis. De la ley al derecho. 2. ed. México: Porrúa, 2005.

VIGO, Rodolfo Luis. La injusticia extrema nos ES derecho. 1. ed. Buenos Aires: La Ley: universidad de Buenos Aires.Faculdade de derecho, 2006. 1. v. Reimpresión

VIGO, Rodolfo Luis. Perspectivas ius losó cas contemporâneas: Ross, Hart, Bobbio, Dworkin, Villey, Alexy, Finnis. 2. ed. Buenos Aires: Abeledo-Perrot, 2006.

VIRGOLINI, Julio E.S. Crímenes excelentes: Delitos de cuello blanco, crimen organizado y corrupción. Buenos Aires: Del Puerto, 2004. (Colección tesis doc- toral 2).

VOLTAIRE. Cartas losó cas. Traducción y notas Fernando Savater. Barcelona: Altaya, 1993. (Grandes obras del pensamiento v. 7).